Gardening
with
Friends

Books by George Schenk

Rock Gardens

The Complete Shade Gardener

Gardening with Friends

Gardening with Friends

George Schenk

HOUGHTON MIFFLIN COMPANY

Boston · New York · London

1992

For information about permission to reproduce selections
from this book, write to Permissions, Houghton Mifflin Company,
215 Park Avenue South, New York, New York 10003.

Library of Congress Cataloging-in-Publication Data
Schenk, George.
Gardening with friends / George Schenk.
p.   cm.
ISBN 0-395-60976-3
1. Gardening.   I. Title.
SB450.97.S35   1992   91-42434
635 — dc20   CIP

Printed in the United States of America

Book design by Robert Overholtzer

MP 10 9 8 7 6 5 4 3 2 1

For my mother
and Holly

Contents

Introduction

My life of peregrination places me now and again in deep suspicion with immigration officers at airports. But fellow gardeners will listen to my story with understanding, I know, or at least I hope.

Since 1977 I've lived mainly abroad, without the fixed address sacred to bureaucracy and constabulary, as a sojourner in several places where I have friends but no property of my own. Yet I garden everywhere I go, as rewardingly as I did during the three decades when I was a home gardener with acreage near Seattle — property sold when I retired from the nursery business.

For the determined gardener that I am, a life of landlessness might have amounted to a Flying Dutchman existence of ghostly detachment. Friends have come to my rescue. In my travels, I visit friends whose properties are clearly in need of my improving hand, or so I convince them. At present there are eight gardens in the world that I have made mine in which to work improvements, properties located in the Pacific Northwest of the United States and Canada, in the Philippines, and in New Zealand. By neat coincidence these gardens number two in each country. In the course of the year I visit all landfalls, devoting about four months each to the North American continent and the two archipelagoes.

Life, despite the frequent jetting across ocean and sea, remains as down to earth as only gardening can make it. In fact, this gardening life of mine provides an even greater attachment to the planet than gardening usually affords. It fosters an acquaintance with plants native to all latitudes and life zones, from the Arctic tundra down through the tropics to wind-scoured subantarctic islands, and a comradeship with people whose cultural heritages, translated into plant terms, are as worlds apart as ginger and gladwyne. That is to say, some of my friends are of Asian and some of British ancestry.

How intermingled are people and plants in the life of a gardener, or so I find it. I could not if I tried place one or the other first in my world. When I depart from one garden theater, the people and the plants I leave behind linger in my mind with a perfectly balanced nostalgia. When the time nears for my return, I anticipate with an equal eagerness the plants and the people I will find at my destination.

It may be just as well that my friends among humankind around the world — friends who are in the main casual about gardening and not devoted to the literature — will probably never read my confession. After all, who would want to be left wondering whether he or she had second billing to a plant? Nobody — including me.

Human sensibility taken into account, it may be just as well, too, that I will probably never know whether I am invited back more for my hale fellowship or for my readiness to plant and weed, water and prune — especially to prune.

I have discovered that I am royally welcome for my ability as a garden sawyer, an ability apparently in undersupply just about everywhere. It helps that I have a certain reputation, relayed from friend to friend, for being able to discipline plants without having them come out of it looking brutalized. My friends, one and all, are rather touchingly baffled over the second great unknown in gardening, which comes after "What to plant?" — and that is "How to keep it in bounds?"

Here, then, is the means by which I often gain garden entrée: I offer to shape up any overgrown shrubby plants. Job done, the relieved appearance of the property may so excite my friends' gratitude and enthusiasm that I am emboldened to suggest further improvements, land-hungry as I always am. My garden friends tend to be minimalists who have planted sparsely. I offer to add plantings in the place of boring blank stretches of lawn, and pot gardens to bare terraces and decks. Yes indeed, I hasten to assure my friends, I will certainly come back and help keep up the new garden. Oh no, thank you, I couldn't accept any remuneration. I'll go ahead and take care of everything. My reward is in the doing, along with such perquisites as home-cooked meals and a place to stay. The perquisites are never particularly mentioned. All is light and easy, an addendum to friendship, with very little bespoken.

When I try to write it down in seemly words, all this unsecured and floating niceness still sounds as if it were being nudged along just a bit by the touch of a confidence man. There may be, at that, in this modus operandi of mine, a certain amount of the Man Who Came to Dinner, with the difference that I don't sit around the house much. I am more the Man Who Comes to Garden. And I will claim that my audacious gardening has added to my friends' lives considerable pleasure and a certain amount of osmotic interest in horticulture.

I would like you to meet this extended garden family of mine, both the people and the plants, in the pages of this celebration of garden friendships.

1

Vancouver
Springtimes

VANCOUVER, APRIL 26. Having landed in this city at the height of springtime, after thirty hours of airplanes and airports on the way from Auckland, I'm like a schoolboy escaping into spring vacation, yahooing out the door and into the air of this most coaxing of seasons. Vancouver, among cities, is particularly generous with its gifts of the spring season. Of the spring seasons, I should say; there are, in my count, four distinct springtimes here. Three of these occur simultaneously: the springtimes of streetside gardens, of botanical gardens, and of woodland reserves within the city bailiwick. The fourth, montane spring-time, is delayed by elevation.

While many of the world's major cities offer the first two, or even three, of these presentations, Vancouver's follow-up springtime is available nowhere else so close to a center of civilization. Mountains rise immediately behind the city's north shore; a twenty-minute drive from near the waterside places one up in a world of plants, climate, and calendar sharply different from that below. Since I have always counted spring-viewing to be among the most educative activities in a gardener's life, I'd better get cracking at the city's four great vernal universities. There will be much to see before the month is out and the earlier flowers fade.

The trip home from the airport with my garden friends, Norma and George, Candida and little Diana, provides ample opportunity to study from our passing car the inner-city springtime of curb-strip and front-yard plantings.

Oh, yes, I'm home again, to the floral realm in which I was born. Although that happened to have been in Seattle, below the border, the international line dividing this natural region counts for nothing in the light of spring. From Vancouver south to Portland, Oregon, urban gardening provides the eye the same extravagance at left and right along the streets. And my appetite for spring is such, I can relish even this floral debauch, visually comparable to an overload of gooey bonbons.

Rhododendrons, a regional specialty, are now full blown, in pink, white, ruby, rose, amethyst, cream, canary, and magenta, and in many blends of those colors, to be seen on whoppers standing as much as ten feet tall and twice that in width in front of older houses. In some front yards, rhododendrons smother the property. In others, the gardeners have pruned away lower limbs to make a handsome evergreen tree of the shrub, one nicely in scale even in those yards, commonplace here, that are as narrow as thirty-five feet. The large-leaved, large-flowered rhododendron hybrids favored for front planting perform best in full sun in this often cloudy region: sun induces compact, rounded growth and a floriferousness that almost totally conceals the plant within a cumulus of color. If you happen to like the particular color, a rhododendron of elephantine size, stupendously in bloom, is one of the great horticultural sightings. If you dislike the color, the effect is more that of a painted elephant staked in front of the house.

Profligate with rhododendrons, Vancouver provides an equal show in another Pacific Northwestern feature, the front-yard rockery. Where streets cut into hillsides, homeowners have kept the resulting embanked soil at the roadside from eroding onto sidewalks by installing rockeries, thousands of them. In springtime, these add up to a citywide floral wassail raucous with basket-of-gold; magenta, rose, and violet aubrietas; evergreen azaleas, most commonly of a funny-paper red; bluebells; tulips in nearly the entire spectrum; and perennial candytuft of an unendurable white glare, from which the eyes shy away self-protectively.

On front lawns, lilacs, just now opening, join the round white or salmon pink eastern dogwoods, the gorgeous golden-chain trees, and the beef-liver leaf forms of plum trees and maples. As seen from a passing vehicle, all these, and other colorful blotches, stand isolated, one by one by one, on the narrow properties. It is the year's main attack of the old malady, spots in the garden, which comes of planting by ones, a dab of this and that; the whole city has come out in multicolored measles. Well, not entirely. We passed a little front yard planted to nothing but lawn along with three golden-chain trees — an actual grove. Wonderful; a unity instead of a spot, a color kingdom in itself. Then came a mile-long boulevard of mature beeches of that aforementioned livery leaf color, which horticulture has discovered in so many kinds of plants, propagated diabolically, and inflicted on springtime. And yet this boulevard parade of beech trees, all of the same unnatural leaf, seemed a thing of hosannaed splendor. I don't know what perverse laws of optics and art prevail here, but I find that leaf or flower colors that are to me bilious in small amounts — on the single plant — can be supremely beautiful en masse.

During these last days of April, I have continued my work as a spring-viewer in the company of garden friends. We found quite another springtime unfolding in Vancouver's Van Dusen Gardens, with its British heritage of plants brought from all over the planet and arranged in freeform groves, lawns, and beds, as pastorally as can be in an urban botanical park. To Britain, a hip-hip-hurrah! No other place since the heyday of Babylon has been such an importer of, and designer with, exotic plants. The excitement of the task, the bounty of plants, and the naturalism of design have all been passed along to form a basis for horticulture wherever English is spoken as a national language. Vancouver offers, in Van Dusen Gardens, one of my favorite British garden retreats in the world, equal in its way to Kew or Wakehurst. Certain areas in Van Dusen are so homey, I relax into a feeling that the garden is my own. (But then, if you read through to the end of the book, you will find I have a rather easy way with that illusion in all kinds of properties.)

I always try to visit Van Dusen on a weekday, better for daydreaming of proprietorship than the weekend, with its crowd. As a further benefit of a weekday outing, you gain the impression that a world lightly populated takes cordial note of your presence. My friends and I visited Van Dusen on a Tuesday, taking sandwiches, a Thermos, and more. We picnicked on the garden's vast hillside lawn, which offered sheltering Douglas firs and distance from the few strollers on the paths, whom we accepted graciously as tourists in our personal principality.

Later we strolled the paths, we few of an elegantly rare species, and stopped time and again for the marvelous, such as the shrub *Paeonia lutea,* nine feet of softly green branches holding out yellow cups, a server of some ethereal drink. Farther on we found a dove tree (*Davidia involucrata*), twenty feet tall at about the same number of years from seed, massed with thousands of flowers, as many as the leaves of the tree, which were just opening. The flowers of this Chinese tree are a celebrated oddity in horticulture, clear white and sizable, fully as big as a dove and vaguely of that graceful bird's outline. Just as vaguely, yet evocatively, the flowers suggest those of dogwood, with white bracts surrounding a central boss of true, minute florets. But in the dove tree's flowers, the two bracts at the top are much abbreviated and the one at the bottom is extraordinarily elongated: a dove's tail. Dove trees like a maritime climate suitable for rhododendrons, humusy soil, full sun,

7

and breathing space all around the crown. The first of several introductions of the tree to gardens in the Western Hemisphere was in the form of seed sent from Szechuan to a nursery in France in 1897, by a missionary from that country. A single seed germinated two years later and gave rise to a vigorous sapling. Early in the twentieth century, cuttings of the young tree were rooted and sent to Paris's Jardin des Plantes, London's Kew Gardens, and Boston's Arnold Arboretum (where that original American *Davidia* still grows).

One thing else, which I hesitate to tell: To some viewers of less buoyant imagination, the tree in flower recalls not the fluttering of doves but the flapping of wet wash on the line. They have given the names handkerchief tree and laundry tree to the noble *Davidia involucrata*. May the goddess Flora forgive them slowly.

Van Dusen's trough garden display is just now in full fig, to use a grotesque but catchy British gardenism, for which I may also be in need of forgiveness. Trough gardening is a recent British invention, mainly postwar, which has caught on increasingly in North America, Australia, and New Zealand.

For me, the troughs themselves, the true articles, provide about half the visual value of trough gardening. The true ones come from England (or, more usually, remain in England), where in past centuries they were used as farmyard or farmhouse basins. Hand-hewn from hard sedimentary stone, they are usually two to three feet across, a foot or a bit more high, oblong or square, or oblong with one of the long sides bayed. The enthusiasm of gardeners for these old basins has raised their value to that of costly antiques. Van Dusen has a fine collection of the real McCoy: stone basins imported from Yorkshire many years ago by an early fancier.

Van Dusen also has the best fake troughs I've ever seen, if one must see such. I would rather not, but I understand their existence. While interest in troughs has grown intense, real ones have become nearly unobtainable, at any price; ergo, artificers have found ways.

In all the parts of the trough-gardening world I've mentioned, professionals and amateurs are at work making cement troughs. Some mix peat moss in with the cement or etch striations along the outer walls of the trough before the cement hardens, but none of this really helps much to naturalize the product. Time, however, and the eventual growth of mosses and lichens, finish the job admirably. In ten years, or even fewer, the cement usually grows sufficiently furry or encrusted to resemble natural stone closely enough for one to dismiss the difference and concentrate on the plants being grown in the trough.

Trough gardeners plant any of about a thousand choice alpines, and very often a treelet of some sort — perhaps a miniature variety of a conifer — to pull the composition together. The usual rooting medium is a scree of crushed stone, humus, and loam, in equal or unequal proportions. Nearly every grower mixes it differently, and many swear by exotic kinds of humus; others abhor the use of any loam at all but will add a helping of sand. As usual in an early and experimental garden science such as this, there is considerable eye of newt and toe of frog hocus-pocus applied to it. Almost any of the porous mixtures that we witches and warlocks of trough gardening (I, too, am a practitioner) provide our plants will produce healthy growth and fine flowering for a year or two on the available nutrients in the mixture. But afterward, most trough gardens decline, the plants wizening because the gardener neglects to add fertilizer, on a misunderstanding that alpine plants necessarily lead a spartan life. Actually, mineral food in plenty seeps down to the roots of plants in mountain crevices and screes. They require something of the same in the garden — an addition of liquid fertilizer (5-10-10 or 10-15-10 or almost any other formula) about once a month from spring until late summer.

I spoke of dismissing the imitation trough with an "oh, well" and concentrating on its contents. I guess I'll never come to a full reconciliation with such cement works, and will always see them as one with false brick sidings, or poured driveways with a pressed-in pattern purporting to resemble cobbles. Depressing trumpery. There is no need of it in trough gardening, for one does not need a trough. A handsomely designed wooden planter, treated to resist decay, works just as well and is the real thing, imitating nothing. So are the large, block-shaped stoneware pots now being made for alpine container gardeners by several professional potters in North America: the real thing, original art. This kind of ceramic plant container will winter without breaking in harsh climates. It is expensive. But gardeners are always the red-hot spenders, lining up at the checkout counters of garden centers on spring weekends as fervently as bettors at a horse race.

Away from Van Dusen, now, into the forest, back on the trail of the four springtimes. A third manifestation of the season opens softly in Vancouver-area woods, refuge of Pacific Northwest wildflowers I have known since I was a tot of four years tramping the woods near my home. Once a nature boy, forever imprinted, like one of Konrad Lorenz's goslings. Those early meetings with plants and flowers, and all else in the wilderness, have proved so deeply indelible, they have directed my course as naturalist, gardener, and garden writer. I often wonder how things might have turned out if I'd been confined to sidewalks early on. But let that be.

Time now for the woods, and for greeting some of my oldest friends in the plant kingdom — the massive bigleaf maples (*Acer grandiflorum*), now seasonably dressed in chartreuse young leaves and pale yellow racemose flowers (source of the most delicate honey that the bees make in this part of the world). A friendly nod to thimbleberry (*Rubus parviflorus*), a canebrake with maple-cut leaves and white wild-rose flowers. From the number of flowers, one calculates the quantity of delicious, raspberry-like fruits to come (in August). Another to the western bleeding-heart, *Dicentra formosa,* springing to leaf and flower at the edge of the thimbleberry patch — a broad colony of light green, lacy leaves forming a level canopy; rising above the foliage, translucent stems topped with clusters of lavender hearts. In all, a lightness.

The plant appears evanescently delicate but is a great survivor. The western bleeding-heart is one wildflower that does not totally retreat from where land developers open the woods with roads and building lots. It clings to any scrap of its old habitat, ready to advance by seed into the cleared soil of roadside and civilized lot, even out in full sun. By ancient habit the bleeding-heart is a first comer into freshly opened soil at wood's edge — a "pioneer plant," as botanists say. Other pioneer plants, such as dandelion, plantain, buttercup, and the like, are better known as weeds. Indeed, the bleeding-heart often shows up as a seedling weed in vegetable and flower beds, but unlike the others is extremely easy to oust, requiring only the lightest tug at its crown, though something more of a pull at one's conscience for betraying an old friend.

Western bleeding-heart is one of the parents of such popular hybrids as *Dicentra* 'Bountiful' and *Dicentra* 'Luxuriant', bestowing stamina and longevity on the garden-born plants; their other parent is turkey corn, *Dicentra eximia,* of eastern North America, a clump-forming species of short duration, which has given its rosy color to hybrid offspring. The garden plants far exceed their wildflower parents in showiness and in extension of flowering season: April through September, in the case of 'Luxuriant', when the plant is grown in moist, fertile soil. The western parent begins its production in early April, with a great show of flowers, and brings down the curtain in fully unrolled foliage by about mid-May; but then this bleeding-heart is a great taker of curtain calls, with floral stems poking out through the green drapery in ones and twos for weeks after the closure of the spring show.

I think I have never so appreciated the cool lavender of this plant as on this day in these woods. It is a color that wears well, with a soothing quality more lastingly welcome than that of the rosy hybrids or, I must admit, of *Dicentra formosa* 'Bacchanal', my own burgundy red selection of the species (which is at least tenuously established in the Scottish and English nursery trade, if not in the American).

Norma and Candida, my companions in spring-viewing, charmed by the lavender bleeding-heart, asked if it would last in a vase. I answered yes, after casting back a good half-century in memory to the last time I had picked any. Since this species remains common, even close to the city, I raised no environmental outcry when my friends began snipping off the fragile stems of flowers.

Standing by, I reran a very old mental movie in which the bleeding-heart figures. The flower was one of those Mayday victims of us grade-school children, sent forth with evangelistic exhortation by our teachers toward the woods and fields to pick wildflowers: an apparently holy task assigned to children on this day. We brought back dandelions, spring queens (*Montia*), and bleeding-hearts, all strangling and expiring in our hot grip, to be placed in a paper-and-paste basket of our own making — a piece of work as tragic, in a miniature way, as a job of wallpapering by Laurel and Hardy. The gasping flowers in the collapsing baskets were to be presented to our parents or neighbors later that day. Bleeding-hearts received and placed in water by a kindly parent revived well, I recall.

Vancouver's fourth springtime, special to this city, takes place in mountains so close you can stand on their shoulders and look down into town at a steep angle. The spring-watcher, in driving up into the mountains, goes backward toward winter at a rate of a month for about every 1600 feet of elevation. (That's an equation I've worked out over many years, employing knowledge of what goes on at a given time in spring with key plants in the lowland that also grow in the mountains.) Having ascended to that first demarcation, 1600 feet, on the calendar day April 30, we reached the montane end of March. At this elevation, red-flowering currant (*Ribes sanguineum*), in the lowland well past flower and on toward summer leaf, was aburst along every branch with pomegranate red racemes, a visual effect like that of popping corn.

This is a roadside flower of "Stop the car!" attractiveness. It is a smallish shrub, about head-high, you find when standing beside it. The branches are now tufted, amid the flowers, with pale little bows of beginning leaves. A musky fragrance, rather like that of osage orange, is exhaled from the flowers and infantile foliage — a scent intolerably strong to the boy that I was long ago, but now the senescent nose finds it faint and pleasant.

The irradiant red of the blossom is of a hue unique

in the native flora. I have long entertained an idea that the flower invented itself as an invitation to red-loving hummingbirds, which also arrive in April, ardently hungry from their long northward migration. The flower, a waiting banquet, signals with its simulation of ruby plumage: Come and sip nectar; carry pollen when you go.

Gardeners in the British Isles receive *Ribes sanguineum* almost as gratefully (trust me on this) as our hummingbirds do, for while the plant remains a collector's rarity in North America, many Britons admire it as one of the finest garden gifts of early spring. Color forms of this variable western American species offered by English nurseries in the nineteenth and early twentieth centuries were of a pale pink wash, evidently a disappointment to many, as one reads in the writings of Vita Sackville-West. More recently, seedling selections made in England provide deeper shades. Curiously (to me), the most popular of these, *Ribes sanguineum* 'King George', is a lifeless, dark, dull red, not at all the vibrant vermilion of North Vancouver's mountainside plants, but pale pinks also flower here in the mountains. Who knows, different hummingbirds may be differing connoisseurs.

Going up. At 2200 feet — mid-March — we found shrub alders, their branches still a leafless winter frame, yet repellently beautiful with flowers over which one cannot make up one's mind: eight-inch tassels of cornsilk yellow, dangling like a thousand stretched-out earthworms somehow turned floral. A scrubby grower, the alder is as showy and shocking as that famous tassel-bearing shrub of late winter, *Garrya elliptica*. I must try to root cuttings, or collect seed, of the best form of the montane alder. If it retains its compactness, the plant will make a first-rate addition to the late winter garden. As for the *Garrya*, I grew it for about fifteen years, and was grateful when a winter of near-zero temperatures in the Pacific Northwest relieved me of it. I had never come to agree with the enthusiastic write-ups I'd read in gardening books, but found that the shrub's sizable evergreen leaves always corroded to shabbiness during winter, detracting greatly from the flowers opening in their midst.

Above 3000 feet our mountain was still winterbound in deep snow. The earliest touches of spring had reached, on this April 30, the vicinity of 2700 feet — late February, as I calculate it on the flower calendar. Here at the ragged edge of the retreating snow, that gloriously stenchy arum *Lysichiton americanum* had arisen from its muddy sleep, vigorously thrusting bright yellow candles from the beds of snow-water runnels.

I wonder if there is for each of us a remembered first flower in life? This one is mine, and goes back to the beginnings of memory, when we were little Indians, my pal Kendal and I, scarcely more than twice the height of this Indian club of a flower. We found it blossoming in a bog, and slogged out and stood beside it, disbelieving that it could be there, so huge, so hotly yellow, an uncanny cleanness above black ooze. The flower awed us into a hushed standstill. For the minute before we turned into wanton boys again and snapped the flower from its mudbound

16

root, to march homeward, warriors with trophy, we shared a response kindred to that reverence of Orientals for the lotus flower, and encountered the mystique of religion for the first time I can remember.

Lysichiton americanum is known to country people throughout its California-to-Alaska range as skunk cabbage, not totally without cause. I myself don't find the plant bothersomely malodorous, merely a whiff of collard greens robustly boiling. Apparently British gardeners have never been bothered, either, for the species, imported by plant explorers, has long been an admired early bird of the British horticultural springtime and a prestigious item of country gardening. It takes planting in a bog, or along the margin of a slow stream, or in a fennish pasture, to fetch forth the shining green, Jumbo-ear leaves to their full three feet in the weeks after the fleshy flower candles melt down in dissolution. So the plant, called in Britain by its botanical name, has an aura of country gentility added to its aroma. On the West Coast of North America it remains simply skunk cabbage, a thing few can imagine cultivating.

That is a piece of an old and odd story in horticulture, a head-shaker. The *Lysichiton* is one of a number of western American plants that have gone to England (a consimilar climate, to their liking) and gained fame, while they remain scarcely known at home. The western gardener conversant with native plants who also goes to England will find old friends everywhere, even toward the center of London: the red-flowering currant, for one, in the window-boxes and marquee planters of banks, hotels, pubs, ministries, and other buildings, as an ingredient in minuscule yet amazingly rich container landscapes, which blend it with white-flowering *Potentilla fruticosa,* white pelargoniums, dark fuchsias, hebes, and osmanthus, for spring-to-fall flowering. Hard pruning keeps order in such lushly landscaped containers. Then, our native thimbleberry, of the white single roses in our springtime woods, blooms also at Warwick Castle, in the English Midlands. Our western bleeding-heart, the lavender *Dicentra formosa,* seems entirely Victorian amid summer annuals set out early on the balconies of Kensington Palace's Sunken Garden.

My tour of duty and devotion as a spring-viewer is now fulfilled. It is good to have got home in April, the best month for a northern gardener's yearly rebirth, along with all the up-and-coming plant life. It is a time to review and to plan, as surely as the garden grows in the mulch of the gardener's experience. That, for me, is the message of T. S. Eliot's most celebrated stanza, the one I'm always going around reciting at this time of the year, to the undoubted annoyance of my friends:

> *April is the cruelest month, breeding*
> *Lilacs out of the dead land, mixing*
> *Memory and desire, stirring*
> *Dull roots with spring rain.*

2

Gardening
on a Railing

Lᴏʀᴅ, ʜᴏᴡ ɪ ʟᴏᴠᴇ a railing! A railing located anywhere I can get at it: a railing at the edge of a deck, or a railing on a balcony or terrace; a railing broad and strong enough to support plants in containers. I love a railing even better than a plant table, because the railing is usually higher, bringing small plants closer to eye level, elevating them to major garden importance. With a line of container plants upon it, a railing becomes the Orient Express of gardening adventures, a train of enchantments.

Say hello to Diana of the railing garden, nine and a half, daughter of my garden host and hostess, George and Norma, of North Vancouver. I barely heard the slight whooshing sound of the sliding door that leads out onto the deck, and suddenly there the young lady sat, lost in thought, oblivious to my activity. A moment later she was gone. Darting appearances and disappearances are characteristic of Diana, whose sudden ways remind me of a chipmunk. For the moment, her presence provided a focus for the garden, like one of those old-fashioned statues of Diana the Huntress, or of Psyche, or of whoever in the classic pantheon, poised in a niche at the end of a garden vista.

In another role, Diana is the vital presence in this garden. She is the water-bearer to fifty-six assorted pot plants. Some of the plants on this open, sunny deck require watering every morning, or even twice daily in hot, windy weather. Most days there is nobody else around to take care of the chore. Her parents both work, and I am away most of the time. Happily, Diana is unusually reliable and thorough about the watering. I'm so grateful that I insist on giving her the grand stipend of twenty-five cents a day, which she accepts with a graciously reluctant gladness.

All this fuss is for the benefit of only fourteen drought-sensitive plants in the collection, which really need daily watering. But these plants are the dancers and singers in the garden, the bright flowers and the airy leaves. Preponderantly, the display is of weightier, sculptural plants, in the form of cacti and a few succulents.

Cacti are a main gardening interest, a fascination, of Diana's and of her mother's. There was a time in my own life — I was about Diana's age — when I too was mad for cacti and would buy them at our local five-and-ten-cent store the way other children bought candy, whenever I had the coin. That boyhood interest departed as I grew. Now it returns, as a reflection of my friends' wonderment over these vegetative sculptures, whose variety is perhaps equaled in the macroscopic world only by seashells.

Diana, appreciative of the tiniest differences in cacti, has recently guided me around the railing garden on a connoisseur's study tour of the kinds and colors of their spines: reddish fishhooks cunningly concealed beneath a silky pelt, as with certain trout flies, in the cactus species *Mammillaria bocasana*; a pale yellow peach fuzz (glochids, technically) arranged in dots on the pads of *Opuntia micro-dasys*; starfish, stony gray, spread out thin-legged upon the ribbed surfaces of *Ferocactus* species; dandelion seed parasols, feathery white and soft to the touch, crowded on the domes of *Mammillaria plumosa*.

Diana, her mother, and I drive to garden centers in search of another and yet another of these exiles from the deserts of the Americas. When we get home, I tip the cacti out of their plastic nursery pots, arrange them in better-looking terra-cotta ones, and place them out in the sun on the deck — and inevitably out in the rain, which closely follows in the Pacific Northwest climate. The cacti thrive on frequent summer rain, provided their rooting material is loose and gritty and pot drainage is swift.

I do go to extremes about the pots for all the plants in the garden, insisting on ceramic as a matter of looks. I was not born in the age of plastic, nor will I ever enter it any more than I can help, and I can help in the matter of plastic pots. Up with the lid of the garbage can (of plastic, and a great advance on the rattlebang cans of galvanized metal I grew up with) and in with the pots. They will be replaced with clay, glazed or unglazed, of a plain design and an earthy color. Except for the all-too-plain, old-time red clay flowerpots still to be found stacked in many garden centers, decent ceramic pots are not at all common. Even with the thousands of creative potters at work these years, a dignified, unobtrusive pot for growing plants, one that does not shout with colors or shock with suggestively anatomical knobs or is not in some way impractical of shape, is hard to find.

When I do get my hands on the right pot, an idea may flash forth instantly, like an old-fashioned cartoonist's light bulb aglow overhead. I may know at once what I'm going to plant in it. Or I may see and admire a pot and snap it up at the sales counter, but have no immediate idea of what to do with it. In that case, I count on envisioning the planting eventually.

In still other instances, I will have a worthy container in my possession, not knowing yet what to do with it, and the answer will be thrust upon me. Such was the inception of the grove of jade trees (*Crassula arborescens*), grouped in an oblong, Italian-made container that now summers on the deck railing. The pot, shipped from Italy to garden centers around the world, is a dandy in design but a killer to any but succulent plants. Half an inch thick of walls and unglazed, it soaks up literally quarts of water, draws moisture from the contained soil, and quickly brings on drought. Knowing of this proclivity from experience with other thick unglazed pots, I kept this one in reserve until I might acquire some tallish kind of drought-tolerant plant to go in it. The answer was handed to me by a generous garden friend, in the form of several good-sized, rooted cuttings of jade tree. The cuttings were large enough for me to be able to break off branches, which I inserted in the soil of the container to make minor trees in a grove planting in which the major, rooted cuttings form the patriarchs. The smaller cuttings soon rooted, yet their relationship to the larger trees has never changed — they've never grown up — in the twelve years since the grouping was put together.

There is much visual entertainment in the railing garden, whose values come forth in the contemplation of the statuesque calm of the cacti and other succulents, and in the discovery of daily developments in the leafy and flowering plants. Norma tells me that nearly every morning, before she goes to work, she spends a few minutes looking at the plants, thereby leavening her whole workday.

George, I am told, delights in claiming that the garden is his, idea, design, technology, and all, whenever he and Norma have guests for a barbecue on the deck and I'm not around. I'm tickled to hear of it. That George, he's a sly one, with only the faintest twinkle that gives away his pawky humor.

There is the matter of the shared name. All my life, I, George, have been meeting Georges and have quickly risen above the slight awkwardness of it — those Georges and I both, suave, adaptable chaps that we are. With my North Vancouver friend and I, being George and George is like membership in some boisterous club, with the name as password. We hail each other, "Hello George!" grandly emphasizing the first *g* and rolling the *r* like a barrel of beer; or we disgustingly smear each other with the peanut-butter-and-jelly version, "Hello, Georgie!" We carry on like this year after year, two adolescents in an arrested state of social growth.

Just now (August), George is drying his garlic crop, which he has spread out on the deck's picnic table. The gray-violet stems and bulbs of the plant glisten with a silky sheen in the sun. His garlic looks gorgeous side by side on the table with pot plants, in a combination that reminds me of an old Dutch still life, not in actual content but in the audacity of the mixture. The rest of George's vegetables — bok choy, scarlet runner beans, tomatoes, and zucchini — fill a twelve-by-ten patch of ground in a corner of the back yard. He has grown vegetables here every year since the family moved into the house.

George tends his vegetables, Norma her flowers: rows of annuals in narrow beds along the walls of the house. His interest in plants and hers divide, as they do so often in husbands and wives, into practical gardening and pleasure gardening, into plants as food for the body and as sustenance for the soul. Fortunately, these gardening polarities blend somewhat in a mental middle ground — vegetables also serve the mind and flowers restore the body — with the resulting garden interplay helping to keep the spouses on speaking terms. George and Norma, for one couple, appreciate each other's efforts, and say so. However, vegetable versus flower gardening can escalate into an ongoing battle of the sexes. I know one couple who have been gardening side by side yet adamantly apart for more than sixty years. He perennially carps that growing anything inedible ("That rubbish!") is an unconscionable waste of time and space, while she perennially nudges her flower planting forward into the beds of soil he tills meticulously for his vegetables. But perhaps this still works out as a kind of "I say tomaytoes, you say tomottoes" duct to contrary love.

Among the pot plants on the deck is a deep green, glossy-leaved shrub at the base of the railing: *Aucuba japonica* 'Longifolia', which, on experimentation, I find to be a great success as a summer deck plant and a winter houseplant. The aucuba goes indoors in early November, outdoors in April. There would be no problem wintering the shrub outdoors, since *Aucuba japonica* in all its varieties is hardy in the Pacific Northwest, but I have found that it makes a wealth of winter greenery indoors, and at a purchase price much lower than that of any of the more usual indoor shrubs of comparable size.

No doubt the showier gold-variegated forms of aucuba would also serve as houseplants. Although I've never cared to plant one outdoors (these plants seem as out of sorts with the out-of-doors as would a contessa in full baroque on a hike in the woods), I can pleasantly visualize gold-variegated aucuba indoors as part of a richly patterned setting, perhaps with Persian carpeting or stained glass windows. Too much? Maybe. Matisse might have loved it, though. I'll give it a try, if ever I add the right room to my garden itinerary.

During a long summer season, and on into autumn, two varieties of *Fuchsia magellanica* enrich the railing garden with their flowers constructed of ruby sepals pendent over a cloche of purple petals: one is the old-timer 'Gra-

cilis', whose main season is July and August, with a sprinkling of bloom for weeks afterward; the other is a newer
clone, 'Papoose', in season from August until October.

'Papoose' is a compact plant with a short, thick trunk.
By thinning the branches yearly, you can turn this variety
into a miniature weeping tree that is greatly charming
when in flower. I'm being careful not to apply the term
bonsai, since my plant has no such premeditation. Yet
nearly everyone who sees the little tree in flower uses
that word, as in this verbatim huzza: "A fuchsia bonsai!
I've never seen one before." The plant's older brother,
Fuchsia magellanica 'Gracilis', makes a pot shrub with several trunks and no bonsai pretensions whatever, yet with
such an abundant rain of Cupid-dart flowers in antique
fuchsian two-tone that the thing looks as if it fed on a
mulch of Victorian valentines.

Both fuchsias are wintered by taking them out of their
pots in the autumn. The surely hardy 'Gracilis' is simply
set out in the ground, a little deeper than it grew in the
pot. But the uncertainly hardy 'Papoose' is completely buried, in order to protect its trunk and branches. My technique is to cut back the roots and branches by one third
and then to bury the plant, remaining crown and all, below the likely level of winter frost, in the light, airy loam
of the open garden.

I had grave doubts the first time I tried this with 'Papoose', which had come to be one of our best-loved pot
plants. Would I recover it alive, or was this experiment
going to turn into an embarrassment and a guilt? Certainly

it was an exigent measure, since I had no greenhouse, or even a chill, well-lighted room, or any other place or means of wintering the plant.

As you may guess, I wouldn't be reporting on this if the news weren't good. On my return the next April, I hastened to dig up the fuchsia, and with a winner's thrill I found eager new roots splaying from the stubs of the old ones and equally eager sprouts springing from most of the previous year's stubbed branches. I've repeated this burial and recovery in two additional seasons, and feel sure about it by now.

In May and June, before the fuchsia season, a miniature bulb flower, *Rhodohypoxis baurii* 'Picta', provides a potful of color on the deck railing. It's not really a bulb; a corm, rather, technically similar to a crocus in its underground food-storage vessel. Although the plant is much smaller than a crocus in its flower, it is considerably more engaging, if I may judge from the sentimentality with which all of us here seem to regard it. We grow the *Rhodohypoxis* in a shallow (three-inch-high) oblong bonsai pot, where it opens a jostling crowd of flowers, like a flock of small butterflies, all of a kind, gathered to drink at a moist spot of earth. The flowers have hidden centers and show nothing more than six elliptical petals, pinkish white, atop a stem approximately the length of one's little finger, hidden beneath the flower.

The *Rhodohypoxis* in their pot pre-date the railing garden. It was about ten or twelve years ago, as nearly as I can remember, that I planted the corms, barely covering them with sandy, gritty loam. For at least a decade the flower show has come back yearly, growing showier as the corms have increased. Flowers, multiplying apace with the corms, numbered well over a hundred this year.

For the past couple of years, though, I've been concerned that I must be letting the plants become criminally crowded in their pot, with the likelihood that fewer and smaller flowers will open next year. The next year comes, and 'Picta' continues to confound with still more flowers, as big as ever. But I really think it would be folly for me to press my luck further. Next spring, for sure, I'll divide the plant while it is still dormant.

Clearly, *Rhodohypoxis* is capable of thriving undivided for a very long time in a pot, even on the shallow, cramped supply of soil in the container I've given it. We do fertilize the plant frequently with the same stuff in an eyedropper bottle we give all the deck's plantings. I'm tempted to name the product, a well-known, aquamarine-tinted, 10-15-10 fertilizer sold throughout North America, but I won't. I've always doubted that it could be a permanent, well-balanced diet, since the label lists no trace elements. Yet plants grow and flower year after year on no more food than this elixir. Science makes rules that plants refute.

Rhodohypoxis baurii 'Picta' and other clonal color forms of this white-, pink-, and rose-flowering South African wild flower have in recent years become an abundant offering at garden centers in North America and elsewhere.

This is a new role for the plant: as a commoner. Up until about 1980, it remained aristocratically rare, a collector's alpine available from only a few specialty nurseries, including my own, The Wild Garden. At about that time, this floral sprite got "discovered," in somewhat the way good-looking young women working behind drugstore soda counters are said to have been espied by movie scouts and helped along to lives of razzle-dazzle and the making of millions for an industry.

In a few short years, *Rhodohypoxis* has come up from being an obscure prize to being a bonanza for the nursery trade. I'm always amazed at how swiftly such a transition can be effected in horticulture. I recall receiving, sometime in the 1970s, an inquiry from a national mail-order company: Where can we purchase 3500 each of three varieties (which the letter named) of *Rhodohypoxis baurii?* I wrote back that such numbers were almost certainly not in existence, but suggested the mail-order outfit try a certain nursery in Scotland, which might, I thought, be able to work up that quantity, given time.

Today, the shelves and tables of garden centers stock the plant by the thousands, keeping up with its mounting popularity. Although this plant never had, and still does not have, a common name in common usage, nursery entrepreneurs are nothing if not inventive. Recently I saw *Rhodohypoxis* selling under a brand-new moniker, a name felt-penned onto a placard, stapled onto a stick, and plunged at the front of a flat full of plastic-potted *Rhodo-*

hypoxis baurii 'Picta' in a garden center attached to a hardware store. The placard merely read "June Baby Flowers"; no Latin name beneath, nor any advice on cultivation.

Since there is a trick to keeping the plant alive where winters are wet and frosty, as is the case here, I can only assume that everybody who bought the plants without having any knowledge of them lost them. Even though many California gardeners leave their *Rhodohypoxis* out in the open year-round, as I do myself in the Californian climate of North Island, New Zealand, in colder regions of the Northern Hemisphere the plant is surer to return in spring if its soil is kept totally dry from about late October to about early May. In my nursery years, I induced the desired seasonal desert by transferring the flats in which the plant grew to an unheated garage for the winter. Before making the change to the cold, dry indoors, I waited until the leaves were yellow and the plant well on the way to dormancy. This species is leafless in winter, and then requires no light. Dormant and dry, the plant will survive with perfect ease at temperatures near zero Fahrenheit, as I know from experience in the Pacific Northwest. And I have a hunch that the plant, winter-dry, will prove hardy all across North America.

❁

The Buffalo Garden, a landscape arrangement of cacti in a container summering on the deck, is my tribute to the Old West. The composition is made up of dwarf cacti species growing at the base of sere gray mountains, which are actually buffalo chips. These, as you know, were the coals in the campfires of Plains Indians and westering pioneers.

Some people think I'm kidding with this garden. But none so far told me they find it repellent. Buffalo chips must be generally accepted as decent, and they certainly serve as conversation pieces. This is a much talked-over garden. I've been asked (though not in so many words) where one finds the legendary spoor of the American bison kicking around on the western plains these days. Only in parks and on ranches where the beasts are kept. I picked up my trophies on a buffalo ranch in Montana and, ignoring the howls of my traveling companions, stashed the chips in the trunk of the car for the trip back to the coast. After all, it was my car and the buffalo chips were nicely old and dry. Here was one of those circumstances in which the gardener must take horticultural liberties — the same thing as poetic license.

Toward the end of September, the Buffalo Garden will be moved indoors to winter near a window, in dry condition. I will leave directions once again (before I depart from North America) that no water should be given during autumn and winter, until early February. After a thorough soaking at that time, it will receive no more water until May, when it is placed outdoors for the summer. We will then water the plants occasionally (or Diana will), applying diluted fertilizer with the water. The rest of our cacti collection is treated to this same indoor-outdoor regime, with drought on purpose during the winter, when cacti are dormant and subject to rotting at the root if the soil is moist.

With the Buffalo Garden, the long drought is doubly beneficial, as it forestalls erosion of the Buffalo Mountains. The garden is now two years old, and I hope to extend its life for perhaps two years more, or until the mountains erode into a mulch. That should be sufficient time in which to make of this container garden a full gardening experience and a good memory.

The lifespan of most of my container landscapes, which have totaled many dozens during the second half of this century, is generally not long but long enough. The end has never come as total demise, but as an end to the garden's ornamental value and its effectiveness as a dream machine, often with the failure of just one or two of the crucial plants in a composition containing several. Sometimes I will restore the garden, adding plants to replace any losses. Or I may decide to take it apart and use its healthy components in other ensembles.

Plant losses in container gardening bother me much less than they once did. These are years in which I demand less and less longevity in the plants I grow. In times past I was enamored of the kind of container gardening the Japanese call seikei: the presentation in miniature of heroic scenery and apparent eternity. I worked for these illusions of nature and age, and deluded myself into presuming an illimitable future for the container landscape — which was never to be. Nowadays I'm content with the sure knowledge that I'm composing plants for the short term.

Nor are my container landscapes at all as determinedly picturesque as they were in my seikei days. I care not a jot about creating a believable natural landscape in miniature. Just an impression of nature is what I'm after. That's it! I'm going to call the style impressionistic gardening. The Buffalo Garden fits the definition. So does one other of my compositions on the deck railing.

"George, I can see you're in earnest about this . . ." The words are those of my mother, a redoubtable old dear, whom I had brought by to meet my garden friends, both the two-legged and the rooted. Her voice trailed off, but the mildly dismayed expression on her face completed the critique. It was not the Buffalo Garden that nonplussed my so-proper parent, who said right out that she liked that one. The container garden over which we failed to see eye to eye is the one I call Steamboat Rockery, after a laval mesa known as Steamboat Rock in the coulee country of eastern Washington.

The namesake rockery is a stack of mossy and lichened rocks balanced one atop another. This garden of primitive plants has grown in health for years on a diet of stone, hot sun, rain, snow, wind, and whatever eolian soil particles come to it. All those weather ingredients are necessary to the garden. Lichens and mosses are in most cases fastidious plants. Those found in sun and full exposure (as these were) should be grown similarly. Those species native to shade and shelter must be given like conditions. Steamboat Rockery is never watered or fertilized, which would sicken its native petrophytic mosses and lichens. They love a lean life.

With this garden, I am on a plane above any criticism,

35

since I have received for it one of the higher awards of my gardening career. I was not on hand to accept it in person. Diana has told me of it. The child brought a playmate of hers to see the plants on the deck, of which she is understandably proud, having an all-important hand in their well-being. Diana's friend stood enthralled by Steamboat Rockery, traveling over it visually for a long while, attracted to this above all other plantings on the deck. Such is my interpretation of Diana's report. She, too, likes the garden, though not with the mesmerism her friend seems to have felt. I'm pleased but unsurprised at having gained the approbation of these children. It is, after all, the renascent child in the gardener who practices the art of the container landscape, this seeking of little worlds. That youngster speaks to any others who come along.

3

Along a Fence

FROM THE second-story deck of our Vancouver garden, one gains visual access to about eight neighborhood back yards evenly apportioned by plain, six-foot-high board fencing stained walnut brown, an agreed-upon neighborhood fence style. Back-yard life is carried on here in somewhat of a tic-tac-toe fence grid. Music arrives over the fencing — from one side, the relentless drumming *lubdub* and estrous lyrics of the popular din of this century's second half, which I still hope to outlive. From the other side, the notes of a Mozart sonatina come a cropper, but bravely get up, dust off the frockcoat, and proceed, the eighteenth century forwarded by a child pianist at practice. The baroque blends with barbecue vapors wafting over the fencing, and soccer balls sail in, to be tossed back politely.

All this becomes acceptable once the mind is made up that the good old days are here and now. The hum of the neighborhood, of humanity at home sharing what is left to us of the country life in this late twentieth century, will no doubt seem a hundred years hence, in a world of high-rises, as pretty as a Grandma Moses painting of village life a hundred years ago. People may yet hang happy pictures of nostalgia entitled *Backyard Barbecue,* or *Children in a Blue Plastic Pool.*

While in a Back East frame of mind, I ask Robert Frost's question about stone walls, but alter it for the suburb: What does all that board fencing keep in or keep out, anyway? Frost's only answer came from his neighbor, as they worked face to face restoring the wall between them: "Good fences make good neighbors." I can see the other fellow's viewpoint, as it applies to back yards here. The roving dog, and nearly everyone else, needs reminding of the exact boundary of the home turf.

In praise of fences, the example at one side of our back yard is a beaut — as board fences go. The lumber is kiln-dried; the posts are secured at ground level in heavy iron stirrups painted black; the stirrups in turn are fixed in an underground wall of concrete. The subterranean structure follows along beneath the fence to a depth of at least eighteen inches; that's as far as I've dug down in my gardening — without having come to the bottom of the underground wall. The purpose of the hidden concrete, far in excess of that which is needed to support the fence, is prevention of root encroachment from our garden. I'm all for it.

The neighbors installed this excellent fence and underground partition and have planted their side attractively with flowers. On our side I've planted fruit trees on semi-dwarf stock — a McIntosh apple, an Italian plum, and an Oriental pear, which is a shapely tree and bears a favorite fruit of my friends. The fence faces north, but the heads of the trees stand above the six-foot boards in full sun. In nearly full shade along the fenceline beneath the trees grow edible rhubarb, sweet woodruff, epimedium, Welsh poppy, meadow-rue, and ferns. These are all booming up from a heavily fertilized soil I'm going to tell you about in a moment, in describing my ground work along the opposing, south-facing fence. This north fenceline planting measures only a few feet front to back, yet has the Edenic lushness of a Rousseau painting, lacking only a lion peering from the leafage. Actually, there are leafy lions here, the rhubarb plants, which grandly offset all the other vegetation in the long narrow bed, fine-leaved things, every one. I rate the kitchen rhubarb one of the most useful landscape plants I work with.

At the other side of the back yard (for it is still a back yard, with only my fenceline plantings at the sides and George's back corner vegetable patch alleviating back-yard life in an empty board box) there is a quite different fence, although of the same plain board design. Here George and his neighbor went in together on the cost of the material. They made a serious blunder in not buying the best kiln-dried wood. The boards were not only insufficiently dried but are of five-eighth-inch finished lumber, thinner than that on the other side of the lot. Within several years of installation, some of them had shrunk so much they actually snapped in two, fixed at top and bottom as they were, with no way to shrink except into pieces.

I would like to see this fence taken down sometime

before it is ready to fall, which can't be more than several years ahead — taken down and not replaced. I've encouraged a no-fence future by putting in a planting designed eventually to replace the fence by providing any needed psychological division between the properties, a planting that will look equally attractive from both sides. George and Norma have approved the idea wholeheartedly. I have not spoken to the neighbors about this, a part that is not mine to play, but I have met them and found them to be friendly and admiringly interested in learning the names of the plants I put in — a good sign. The children of both families are well-behaved and not likely to do any bashing of vegetation intermediate to the properties. Neither family keeps pets that need corraling. There is nothing here, as Frost noted in his situation, to be walled out or walled in. Something there is that does not like a wall and wants it down. And so do I.

The bed along this fence, which I dug and planted three years ago, bellies out from the fenceline at an average, undulating width of only three feet. I had to keep it narrow to preserve the main space of the back yard for Diana's swing and for games of badminton. I expect that Diana will outgrow the swing in a couple of years, and then I'll widen the border.

A considerable part of my gardening life, now that I think of it, has been waiting for children to grow into young adults who will move out in the world and leave the yard to me. I would gladly encourage them to trowel down as they grow up, instead of taking over their territory. Yet it happens that no child I've ever known has grown up to be a gardener. And I see evidence, in an increasing daintiness, a fear of angleworms, and an attraction to indoor pursuits, that Diana will prove no exception.

Even so, the little lady was my lifesaver of a garden companion on the June days when I dug this south fence-line bed out of the lawn that covered the ground to the base of the boards. Diana extended her role as water-carrier to include me among the parched horticultural specimens. The weather was unseasonably hot, and each of several days' work sessions of three hours each took about a one-gallon guzzle. No exaggeration. Diana brought me nearly frozen cans of beer, glasses of fruit juice, and pitchers of iced water, as I, as runneled of hide as a draft horse pulling a load of sorghum, labored away in the summer sun. No wonder I put children off gardening, with my Neanderthal appearance and performance. A quiet game of Monopoly probably makes more sense.

The earthwork began with my outlining the bed-to-be with a garden hose. Then I used a spade to cut a line down through the sod, following the hose. Along the outside of the cut, on the lawn to be retained, I laid out an entire twenty-pack box of the largest plastic bags I could find at the supermarket. Next I desodded the area of the bed, cutting out blocks of sod with the spade and stacking them along the farther side of the plastic-bag tarpaulin. Grass removed, I dug out the bed to a depth of sixteen inches. I would have dug deeper had the weather been cooler.

The soil I dug out proved to be the usual leached and infertile upland soil of the Pacific Northwest, a sandy loam containing many granite rocks smoothed by the Ice Age into small loaves and buns. Besides its stone content, the excavated soil was corrupt with fragments of evergreen tree roots and limbs buried by the bulldozer that had cleared the woods away for the building of the suburb. Stones and debris I piled separately on my makeshift tarp. On completion of the excavation, I threw all this material back in, first thing, along the bottom of the hole. On top of the debris I placed the sod, grass side down.

Next, a generous sprinkling of 10-10-10 fertilizer in granular form. (I would have used a fertilizer of almost any numerical combination, depending on whatever I found available at the local garden center in bulk quantity at bulk price; they seem to me comparably effective.) After the fertilizer, I put half the soil in on top of the sod, and along with it a few shovelfuls of henhouse sweepings (rotted sawdust and droppings), which I had also obtained, bagged, at the garden center. Using the spade as if I were blending pine nuts into pancake flour with a spoon, I mixed the soil and the sweepings. Then in with the rest of the excavated dirt; more fertilizer and henhouse; more blending with the spade; all punctuated with frequent gurgling sounds.

I ended up with a bed of healthily loosened and aerated ground, profligately fertilized the way that old-fashioned chemical farmers treat a cornfield, and also the way that nursery-grown plants are chemically charged up in their containers. Whatever I bought and planted here would be right at home.

The loosened soil stood eight inches higher than the bulldozer-compacted soil of the rest of the back yard. I worried about it, and minimized any tendency of the soil to erode onto the lawn by shoveling a little moat in the earth along the grassline and then patting a smooth forty-five-degree slope along the side of the soil incline with the back of the spade blade, and also by smoothing off the top of the bed into a plateau. In its final shape, the narrow, unplanted bed resembled the grave of a very long snake.

The planting was a single day's work. I mocked up the arrangement before actually setting the plants into the ground — set out trees, shrubs, and perennials, still in their nursery containers, along the plateau top of the bed where they were to go. Much rearranging went into the design.

The plant community had as its tallest greenery eight columnar conifers of the variety *Thuja occidentalis* 'Fastigiata', spaced at seven-foot intervals. Between the trees I placed the evergreen shrubs nandina, Mexican orange, and Oregon grape, together with the deciduous shrubs *Fuchsia magellanica* 'Gracilis' and *Vaccinium corymbosum* in variety (the blueberry of morning muffins). In front of the shrubbery went the subshrub *Santolina chamaecyparissus* and such perennials as astilbe, *Dicentra,* and *Centaurea montana.* (The latter proves to be a weedily seeding mistake in the close community of this planting bed, but is tolerated, kept on, because all women flower arrangers who come by adopt a kind of crooning voice on sighting this plant with its blue-violet wheel flowers. Crooning to the *Centaurea,* and to my hoped-for generosity, they ask if the flower might be good for their purposes. It's a fine flower for the vase, I reply; let me cut some for you.)

The more usual placement of columnar conifers, such as the thuja I used here, is in close planting for privacy — as a hedge that requires little or no pruning at the sides. My planting, however, is open-spaced, so that when the fence eventually comes down (let that be a foregone conclusion), neighbors on both sides of the planting will view shrubbery as well as trees. The trees, shrubs, and perennials in the bed are close but not congested. Three years on, I've not yet had to do any pruning.

All the plants have come on fast, with that boost of fertilizer at the start. The second year I added nothing more of chemical food. This third year I have added a surface sprinkle of the same 10-10-10, and I will repeat with an annual addition in years to come.

The planting has already developed into a valued family possession, serving everybody. Norma harvests flowers. Diana "disappears" the blueberries in ones and twos as soon as they ripen. She is swifter than a starling at this. Most gratifying of all to me, this spring when I returned from Auckland, I found that George, the vegetable gardener, had taken an extreme liking to the santolina, a plant for looks and scent but certainly not the salad plate. There had been several santolina plants in the bed; now there are several more. George had clipped many cuttings from the original plants, seemingly of an impossible size for root strike — a foot long, with woody trunks, instead of properly young, eager branches — and had stuck these whole little santolina trees in the ground here and elsewhere on the property. A good half have rooted and are growing on. I'll end on that note of prosperity.

4

Within the Walls

MANILA, SEPTEMBER 12, a day of fun. A fashion photography crew from Tokyo is blustering about in my patio garden today, a temporary takeover as of a patch of lawn by a flock of fossicking birds, noisy and mutually reassuring, quite certain at the moment that the world is their earthworm.

I'm pleased they've chosen my garden as a setting for their pictures, instead of one of the other, sparely landscaped public spaces here at Casa Manila, a re-created Spanish colonial mansion. At the same time, I'll have to admit to a certain ambivalence. Although I garden with the idea of attracting my fellow species to my special territory, once I've brought the people in with my leafy or flowery show, I regard them with mixed joy and apprehension. Will they appreciate or even comprehend my labor of devotion? One doubts: and silently wishes the invaders were away. One hopes: Perhaps someone among them will bless the garden with a pleasant remark, undoubtedly sincere, that will chime in the mind forever. It has happened before. Just a word of simple appreciation, even by a non-gardener, will do, such as "The garden is looking nice," and makes one's work so much the more worthwhile. All right, then. Don't go. Hope rules the day.

As I say, this is fun. Look at the size of that view camera of theirs! It's a microwave on a tripod. The crew's director, with his Voice of God baritone, is putting three exquisitely starved mannequins through a repertoire of postures and walks alien to the human race. Here comes one dressed in what appears to be a loosely fitted white lace tablecloth. For the camera she is performing a reedy, narrow walk, with suppression of any lateral movement of shoulders and hips, straight on in slow motion, like a heron stalking a frog. But oh, what a lovely heron person.

These avian rituals of the fashion industry are taking place just outside my antique shop at Casa Manila in Intramuros: in translation, "within the walls" of the old Hispanic city of Manila. Here I have kept shop and gardened since 1984.

Casa Manila is a carefully detailed re-creation of the regional architecture of the second half of the nineteenth century, built under the aegis of the Ministry of Tourism in the early 1980s. Rooms on the ground floor that would have been day quarters for servants in the old days are, in the reincarnate building, shop spaces. The upstairs is a renaissance of the family rooms, outfitted as a museum of period furnishings. To get it all as right as possible, Casa Manila's architects and curators consulted yellowing house plans and historic photographs that had somehow survived the bombings and firestorms of 1945.

Except for one building, everything of civilization in the dense intramural complex — the shops, the great houses, the little geometrical gardens, the very grid of the streets — was reduced to a cratered jumble in that final year of the Second World War. Those of us who dote on the past cannot, I think, examine photographs of Intramuros as it was up until the bombing, and then as it was immediately afterward, without at least teariness of thought.

The single structure, out of thousands, that survived was the San Agustín Church, just across a narrow cobbled street from Casa Manila. San Agustín Church is a plain hulk of gray stone, hugely homely but beloved (inside this stone box are wonders of decorative woodwork and statuary rendered in ebony and other native hardwood). The religious accept the survival of the four-hundred-year-old church as miraculous. The more analytical might suppose that stone walls yards thick were simply too much for the bombs. And some of us entertain both views.

Quite often on Sundays, wedding parties promenade across the street from the church and arrange themselves in my garden for picture-taking, proud moments for all of us. The train of the arriving bride's gown (trains are the thing, ever since Princess Diana's wedding dress with its twenty-five-footer) dusts a path across the patio garden's granite paving stones. She walks in beauty, the bride of my garden, with her fascinating sweeper. Looking on I have somewhat the sense of laying claim to seignorial rights. Repeat this scene many times, to include years' worth of brides who have swept into the garden for pictures against a background of the neweled detailing of Spanish architecture and the aqueously shining tropical foliage I've added.

Other frequent garden visitors, my guests for at least the time it takes them to walk through, while perhaps registering the fact they are in a pleasantly leafy room, include rubber-sandaled farm families from the provinces of the Philippine archipelago. Foreign businesspeople and diplomats, mainly men in Savile Row–type black worsted, stroll through my garden in the tow of tour guides, on their way to or from air-conditioned meetings; out here in our everyday steaming ninety-five-degree heat, they simmer ridiculously in their suits, as if in a cartoon cannibal's soup. Well-to-do Filipino matrons in couturier clothing of diaphanous lightness waft through my garden like pastel clouds. (Yet sometimes — let me kiss your hand, madam, you've so rededicated the gardener to his task — they pause to study and to discuss the plants in the garden community.) And then a world's worth of tourists come through in ones and twos, or threes or more. I identify the accents of Australians, Japanese, Americans, Germans, Frenchmen, Englishmen, Spaniards, Italians, Chinese, and Russians; others I don't recognize. About once every week, busloads and busloads of schoolchildren pour in for an on-location lesson in their nation's history. I myself may be the historical highlight of their day. "Hi, Joe!" the more audacious among them will chirp, a greeting that merges me

54

with the G.I. Joe of MacArthur days. But of course the kids are innocent of the deeper summoning in a slogan they've inherited.

Welcome to all the above, my transitory guests. One Sunday, however, some quite sinister members of a wedding entourage showed up, having crossed the street from the church. This experience, which truth compels me to tell, took place before the fall of the Marcoses. Relax: No guns were unholstered, and everything turned out all right. I stood grooming plants in the garden, snipping away spent leaves of *Dracaena marginata*, facing the greenery I've arranged against the walls that define the patio garden, my back toward any foot traffic. I was absorbed in my work, but suddenly became aware with a peripheral glance that five or six praetorian guards of the Marcos family stood behind me, watching. Their black uniforms startled me into recalling pictures of the SS: Marcos's élite actually wore shiny black jackboots that might have been Nazi war surplus. These men were supposed to be across the street in the church parking lot, guarding cars and awaiting the emergence of the wedding party of some cousins (I later heard) of the Marcoses. Instead, they had become considerably liquored up and had wandered over looking for entertainment.

They were transfixed on beholding a sight as eldritch as myself actually engaged in — to their perception — lowly manual labor. "Hoy, amigo!" the most aggressive of the group kept saying, in a bear-baiting tone of voice; "Hoy, amigo!" in an attempt to get me to turn around and dance for them, or at least to give an account of myself. I decided my back and my silence were my only defense. It worked. They swaggered onward. Quickly, I had my shop staff close up, in case these heroes came back and took an appropriative interest in some ivory-headed Marian statuette or some Ifugao idol on the shelves.

Now, had I the wit of a paladin in a Hollywood western, who charms the houligan mob with the right words, I might have addressed my jackbooted audience with a story that would cut right through the alcohol to reach some interior shrine of nice guy. "Gentlemen," I might have begun. "Gentlemen, you may wonder how I come to be here. And I will tell you." Or at least I will inform my reader.

The Philippine connection in my life began long ago, in 1962. My home city of Seattle hosted a World's Fair that year. The Philippine pavilion was one of the gems of the exposition, managed by a staff of bright young intellectuals and socialites from Manila. My late father, a gregarious man, also worked at the fair (as a greeter), met the Filipinos, liked them, and invited them all to our house for a party in their honor. And that was the beginning of a passel of friendships. When you know one Filipino, you know many: This anciently insular population has become like a computer system, amazingly interconnected.

But what am I doing here at Casa Manila with pruning shears in my hand? Well, I've always liked old things — hence the antique shop, in a city that is a crossroads of antique cultures, each of which has left artifacts. As for my gardening, I garden here because I am in the first place a gardener and will seize any scrap of space, time, and opportunity to garden wherever I am.

Early on in my Manila life, in the 1970s, I had an opportunity to test my will to garden within severe limits of time and space. The Casa Manila garden is not my first in the city. My first garden was a balcony production, on the eighth floor of a big, run-down postwar apartment building in Manila's Ermita district — not much of an address but within my budget at the time, in this high-rent part of town. The apartment's single attractive feature was an old-fashioned balcony, livably large at about nine by eighteen feet. My instant reaction was, Here's space enough for a complete green environment, a garden room. Although only a couple of hours of direct sunlight reached the balcony, good light irradiated the space much of the day. The lighting and the measurement of the balcony seemed perfectly accommodating, a go-ahead.

As to that other garden determinant, time, I had to give some thought: Would the making of a garden be worthwhile within the time I would be here? I had moved in with the idea that I would be working in Manila six months (I actually stayed seven). It took me the first week of my stay to decide that a half-year's residency was plenty of time to be a gardener.

Assembling the plants turned out to be the well-known pleasure that shopping for plants is anywhere, but with a distinctly Filipino style. Along the streets of Manila, plant vendors push their carts, snarling and maddening

57

the motorized traffic, oblivious to the outcries of drivers, exercising the ancient, never-revoked rights of *provincianos* who come to town to sell their goods. The plant vendors usually travel in pairs, pushing wooden carts as big as an automobile chassis, and laden. Pitting their whole bodies against the loads, they bend hard forward like men straining against a stalled car.

The carts hold a great bouquet of arching palms; *Dendrobium, Vanda,* and other orchids; leafy figs such as *Ficus lyrata* and *F. benjamina*; variegated crotons and particolored dracaenas; flowering hibiscus and bougainvillea — altogether a gridlock of gaudiness in keeping with the street, and a generous offering of the basic material of tropical gardening. The price: the equivalent of two or three dollars each for plants waist-high or taller.

For several weeks, every time I spied plant vendors from my balcony or while I was riding by in a jeepney, I would either dash for the elevator or jump off the jeepney's tailgate, bargain with the vendors, and have them carry yet a few more heavy pot plants into the elevator and out to my burgeoning balcony garden. (If you are not familiar with the jeepney, that automotive beast of all burdens in the Philippines, let me make the introduction. The jeepney is the invention of Filipino mechanics, who, on the whole, are geniuses at restoring and glorifying rust buckets. On the chassis of jeeps dating in many cases from the American army occupation of the postwar 1940s, ingenious mechanics graft elongated cabs with long benches inside, seating for up to twenty compressed passengers.)

By leaps and bounds, I had before long quite a tropical lushness in place, but there was more to come. On a side street just off Mabini, Manila's tourist strip, a vendor of wild ferns waited; he sat on the ground with his back propped against the trunk of a royal poinciana tree. I walked by about twice daily and nearly always saw him sitting there, a man perhaps in his seventies, waiting with patient readiness for about one customer a week. His territory measured fifty feet of curb strip, the shaded space between a pair of the three-story-high poinciana trees, no doubt planted soon after the war.

He sold nest ferns (*Asplenium nidus*) and oak-leaf ferns (*Drynaria quercifolia*), epiphytes he collected in the forested hills of Batangas, a day's trip by bus, as I found out in chatting with him. He used a machete to chop them from the trees, taking care to provide each fern with a quantity of the leaf mold that clung to its roots. I asked him all about it, but much of the technique was evident when I examined the captive ferns. Through the crown of each he poked a length of stout galvanized wire; then he elbowed the wire at the bottom to secure the plant and crooked the wire to the top to form a hanger. At his curbside space, on wires he had strung from one poinciana tree to another, he had lined the great ferns like a kind of frondy laundry, but the effect was a bizarre beauty. He must have worked out some arrangement with the cops on the beat to allow his illicit enterprise. That's the way it's done here, by hundreds of little sidewalk businesses.

I purchased a dozen of his two- to three-foot-wide nest

ferns and three of the oak-leaf ferns, of about two-foot
span. Back at my apartment, I hung the ferns from the
ceiling above the balcony railing and from the railing
itself, with half the width of each plant hanging out, street-
ward, through the bars. In place, they created a forest-
green privacy screening. Viewers from the windows of
other tall buildings perceived only an amazing flight of
ferny wings over in my direction. I myself disappeared behind fronds into a shadowy world of my own making (so I
determined in looking up toward my balcony from the
street). I love to lurk in leafage, and will cheerfully allow
that my proclivity lays me out for dissection by eager
Freudians, like a pickled frog in a freshman biology class.
I'm more of a Jungian myself, more a believer in tribal
dreams than in infantile ones. I come directly descended
from a long line of cave-dwellers, and in my gardens am
only going home.

The reduced daylight on the balcony brought on by
the fern screening diminished the flowering of hibiscus,
but that seemed a fair tradeoff for the privacy I'd gained.
The ferns had been added to the garden *after* the pot
plants, after my discovery of a means of bringing home
these huge hanging plants (by jeepney and driver for hire).
If the ferns had come early on in my composition of the
garden, then I would have been more studious in selecting shade-tolerant shrubbery to go with them. At least, I
hope I would have; can't really claim to have had the exact
knowledge at that early stage of my tropical gardening.
Yet there is an instinct that works here. From my garden-

ing in other climates I had arrived at a rule of green thumb about shade needs or tolerance: Almost any plant with big, broad leaves will prosper in shade. Tropical gardening is replete with such foliage plants, and even by accident, in assembling several species, one brings home a willing shade garden. So in the main I had a garden of easily basking shade plants, such as ornamental taro (*Calocasia*), crotons, and *Thrinax* palms (with broad, divided leaves), along with others, including of course the great ferns.

Every morning I watered, lavishly, the more than seventy pot plants and hanging plants in my balcony garden. It was the time of the dry season (December or January until June or July), which follows the wet season (the rest of the year). These are Manila's two not entirely wretched seasons. I prefer the long wet, which destroys one's shoes but also washes from the air, at least for a few hours after each downpour, one of the world's more serious cases of air pollution. The succeeding long dry is a time of dusty, leaf-browning winds, to be countered with the watering can. The clay pots of my garden shrubbery and the soil within — faded to pale dryness overnight — were filled to the rims and soaked to darkness each morning. The crown center of each of the great ferns received a morning drenching. All plants were given as well a fortnightly application of dilute fertilizer.

After less than a month on the balcony, the oak-leaf and the nest ferns began unrolling infantile fronds, which within several weeks stretched to full size. These big, impressive foliage plants turned out to be easy growers. Nest

61

fern in particular can be successful even in the sordid atmosphere of the inner city. For instance, in Manila's Ermita district, within a small shopping mall open to the street and its traffic-flavored air, grow suspended nest ferns that I've been admiring for about fifteen years; the most vigorous of the group has attained a frond spread of eight feet, about maximum for the species.

One of my balcony's ferns had come from the forests of Batangas with a stowaway tree frog of no more than half a thumb's length. Naturally I named this imp Hop-o-My-Thumb. But I had not been aware of its presence right away. The frog, hunkered and half-hidden in the mass of stipes at the base of the fern fronds, had played at being a green bump, staying motionless in its station during the hacking of the fern from the tree and during the lurching bus ride down the dirt roads from Batangas; had remained quiescent for days while the fern swung on the curb-strip line; and had not budged when I jostled its leafy home into place along the balcony railing. It remained secreted until several mornings later, at the time of the watering of its ferny nest. The camouflage-green beasty blinked, and gave itself away. As I poured water into the plant, and unknowingly over the frog, its eyes closed and performed a little juggle, retreating somewhat into their sockets one after the other and then bulging back with the same one-two rhythm. Afterward, Hop-o-My-Thumb and I made a daily game of it — *I* did, at least. I preferred believing that my green guest blinked as a signal of thanks for the refreshing shower. There were plenty of insects for the frog,

62

so with the addition of water, it had all that it needed for the duration of my balcony garden, the dry season not being the time that frogs urgently require their own kind.

At the end of my seven months' stay in the apartment, the tree frog, still ensconced in the nest fern, exited with the rest of the garden. With the help of friends — homeowners who were glad to receive the healthy plants as gifts — I stacked the lot into the building's venerable Otis elevator, an unnerving old creaker and groaner. One of us held the door open, immobilizing Otis, while the rest of us loaded in the plants. We had to make two trips, holding up the elevator six or seven minutes for each load, time enough to hardboil an egg or a stymied apartment resident. We feigned indifference to fierce looks from standees in the lobby. Couldn't be helped.

In the years since, whenever I have reviewed this half-year's gardening experience, it has ripened in retrospect into purer and purer pleasure. The adventure seems complete, even to communication with wildlife in the garden. Gardening small and even briefly can bring benefits all out of proportion to the apparent limits. And gardening's benison shows up with special clarity against the meaner city surroundings. The plant is one of life's great rescues from the streets.

Only two blocks away from Casa Manila in Intramuros is a city block squared by dirt streets, a patch of pocky ground never rebuilt after the Second World War but occupied by squatters since the late 1970s, as literally millions of people have come to the city from the provinces seeking richer opportunity, but in this crush of humanity have found even less than they had. Their shanties, tacked together out of dismembered packing cases, scraps of sheet metal and plywood, appropriated signboards, and discarded fragments of industrial polythene, present such a dense facade that the shantytown in its entirety resembles, from a little distance, a colossal bale of compacted trash. This is poverty's depth in Manila. Yet many of the shantytown's residents manage to be container gardeners, for whom the cared-for plant ranks somewhere close behind fire, water, and rice among life's necessities. (I have seen this phenomenon elsewhere in the deepest of slums: plants, kept as tonic for the spirit, growing in rusty cans on shanty windowsills in a Rio de Janeiro *favela,* one of my life's great images of hope.)

Manila's shantytown gardeners use a special kind of homemade pot, a local invention formed of worn-out truck or car tires ingeniously cut and then stitched together to form a vase-shaped container, with the tire tread ornamenting the flared rim of the vase. Planted, the pots are placed in the only sunshine that reaches the shantytown, at its street side. The plants sit, or swing if in hanging containers, perilously close to passing vehicles, and would seem irresistible to any passing thief. Yet they remain safe, unmolested for years, the only kind of removable property that can be left out overnight. Pot plants are apparently untouchable here, in an ironic contrast to more affluent cities, such as New York or London, where chains padlocked around the street-side plant may not be enough to keep it secure.

Among the favorite pot plants in my Manila shantytown is a miniature trailer, *Pellionia daveauana,* native to Burma, with thumbnail-sized, scalloped leaves subtly marbled light and dark green and bronze, in shingled denseness, down two feet of cascading stems — there in tire pots hung on wires. The species offers tidy good looks the year round, and also a fresh liveliness of leaf rare in a pot plant that keeps itself pat. *Pellionia daveauana* grows readily from branches, which need only be pinched off and rooted in water. The plant has the easy ways of wandering Jew (*Tradescantia*), though on a smaller scale. In time, I would expect this little Burmese native, as yet uncommon in the temperate world, to become a fixture in as many homes as the omnipresent *Tradescantia* is today. That, I suppose, would be a gain — at a loss of dignity.

The shrub *Schefflera microphylla,* another shantytown regular, is native to Philippine rainforests and is a small five-finger species, not greatly different from the Hawaiian elf schefflera (*S. arboricola*), lately popular in North American indoor gardening. The Philippine plant has a propensity to root along its stems and to ascend if given a firm surface to climb; grown as a shrubby vine, this species eventually sends its vibrantly yellow-green leaves well overhead. In the shantytown, it is grown as a free-stander, its branches often decorated with white shells of chicken eggs, each of which has been opened sparingly at the small end, leaving the emptied shell nearly intact. The shell is then impaled on the shrub by having a twig stripped of its leaves inserted into the aperture. Over a period of time a tallish schefflera becomes an egg tree, bearing fifty or even a hundred white fruits, curiously attractive.

Why? I've never knocked on a door — egg trees always stand near doors — to ask the burning question. But I have pestered my Filipino friends for an answer. Hemming and hawing, really knowing little of such practices of simpler souls, my friends tend to cobble together a general opinion: The egg display is an invitation to good fortune, Do come in. That's a fairly safe surmise, since out of dozens of plant superstitions, ancient but ongoing among Filipinos, the majority have to do with the supplication of fortune, a minor number with the scaring away of misfortune. Egg trees are by no means confined to Intramuros, or to the schefflera. Other kinds of shrubs are so adorned, in any of Manila's poorer districts, and also in the provinces, where the custom probably originates.

Two city blocks, two measures of dirt street, separate the world of the shantytown from that of my patio garden at Casa Manila. Inside the high perimeter wall of Casa Manila's complex of chambers and patios, about fifteen daytime security guards keep the two worlds workably apart. Security guarding is a major occupation in Manila, with more than eight-score listings in the Yellow Pages of the current phone book devoted to companies that hire out guards. Casa Manila's guards are a friendly lot, police-uniformed boys and girls in their twenties, gats holstered at their hips. They are a daily fact of life here, and an important feature in my garden, motile garden statuary coming or going with the changing of the guard, or seated the day long amid the palm fronds. Sometimes the guards ask me the names of plants, and in answering I give a common name — leea for *Leea coccinea,* golden candle for *Pachystachys lutea* — withholding the binomial as being much too pedantic in the circumstance.

The guards work twelve-hour shifts, six days a week (usual with many jobs in the Philippines). Their presence is undoubtedly necessary to keep "hold-uppers" at bay, but I'm unconvinced about their training with weapons. Once a drunk came lurching in and objected to a security guard's request that he check his pistol; the guard drew *his,* fumblingly, and accidentally shot an onlooking Casa Manila electrician in the foot. Later the drunk calmed down and apologized, and the lucky-unlucky electrician hobbled about Casa Manila for the next couple of weeks wearing a thick bandage. He daren't have taken any time off, for his pay might have been bureaucratically delayed, well-nigh forever.

My gardening here is a dodge around the same snafu, an exercise of audacity, as a lifetime of gardening has taught me that garden-making must often be. Had I asked permission of the Intramuros Authority, the bureaucratic ganglion that governs these premises, the answer, I know from experience, would have been about six months in coming, with no assurance of a yes, we understand, we love you — for such a public-spirited enterprise, at no public cost at all. I merely showed up with a jeepney-load of plants one day, and followed it with other loads, counting on the national habit of relaxed acceptance of the fait accompli to let me get on with my gardening unchallenged. And it has gone well these several years.

When I began, the 45-by-45-foot patio outside my small shop was nearly blank, except for flagstones, a functioning well and wellhead (rebuilt from the ruin of an old well), and a lanky and littersome young ylang-ylang tree forty feet overhead, supplying unwanted shade to a patio already darkened by high walls on four sides, and at the same time ingratiating itself by bestowing an impassioned perfume over the patio, the garden excuse for the gawky tree. This is a scent Filipino country girls capture for themselves by placing the tree's flowers, little twelve-fingered paws of yellow-green, in a bottle and then immersing them in coconut oil. In recent years ylang-ylang perfume has become famed as a designer commodity, called by the name of the tree and sold under the name of a European couturier. All this does not soften my feelings toward the unshapely tree that overshades and messes up "my" patio.

I'm more appreciative of the patio's flagstones. They are of a kind known as *petro china,* "petro chee-nay" in local pronounciation: Chinese stone, brought here centuries ago on trading junks. A quantity turned up in bulldozing the war-torn ground for the re-creation of Casa Manila. Petro china paving stones, a finely grained gray granite, are expensive to buy but much sought by wealthy Manilans for home landscaping; in this, the stones are quite like old street cobbles in San Francisco, purchasable history offered at high price to contemporary gardeners.

The 2000 square feet of bare petro china that confronted my gardening consideration should, I quickly decided, be kept mainly the way it was, open, in order to accommodate the groups of schoolchildren and the patio parties that sometimes assembled there. I decided on a perimeter garden, a band of greenery, narrow at places, then wider, along the walls of the building.

As for plant material, I had graduated from pursuing street vendors. I had discovered White Plains, Manila's main pot-plant market, where, side by side, half a hundred small nursery salesyards line half a mile of one side of a thoroughfare. The variety of plants is more extensive here than that stacked in the vendors' carts; the prices are lower. Shopping at White Plains, one hikes along the edge of the treeless street in vicious tropical heat and ducks into this and that salesyard (Perla's Peerless Plants, Ramon's Green Haven), those that appear the lushest and the most saving from the sun. But all are jungly, a half-mile of rainforest in pots with shade netting overhead, where in temperate climates there would be snow-resistant lathing. This long, long strip of richest green is backed by a continuous high and plain stucco wall of tan color. The harmony of the two, rich plants and plain wall, imparts a palpable atmosphere of calm to White Plains. People who work here constantly absorb the salutary atmosphere and seem almost to develop into an emotional subspecies of human, as Indians have done in remote Edens such as the Grand Canyon's Havasupai Gorge, evolving toward an imperturbable race. At the very least, the White Plains plantspeople are uncommonly calm and pleasant, and life in a garden, which is their lot twelve hours a day, six days a week, seems responsible.

That is the way I remember White Plains. I have not been there since a few days before a recent coup d'etat attempt brought tanks, explosions, and infantry precisely to this half-mile strip of greenery and smashed everything to bits. The high, blank wall, seeming from its plantward side to be garden architecture, was on its other side the wall of an army encampment, which came under siege. On television I saw a cratered no man's land and heard of the deaths along the garden side of that wall, where so recently I had walked in such peacefulness. I must mention this but not dwell on it, for danger and uncertainty are undeniably a part of life in Manila, somewhat more so than in the cities of more stable countries. The plant, the garden, is one's respite from the less habitable world, and that is my topic. The White Plains plant row will no doubt be raked smooth and restocked, and will conjure up the atmospherical magic again. And I will rejoin it all, conscious, I will hope, only now and then of the terrible applicability to this place of the words "in Flanders fields the poppies blow."

❁

A better recollection is of my pleasant routine of going back to White Plains once a year to fill up a jeepney with replacement plants for my garden at Casa Manila. On my trips I have found that a jeepney, hired for the occasion, will hold up to a dozen five-foot palms in fifteen-inch pots, and forty or fifty smaller plants besides. That represents a major replacement of plants each year. My garden location requires it, being too shady and muggy to sustain the less sturdy plants — those livelier in color, thinner of leaf tissues, and hence seeming to be more buoyant, which I insist on growing along with the stalwarts among tropicals. The bright-and-light plants are a minor but vital component in the patio garden, raising its personality above that of stolid institutional landscaping. But almost none of these plants will endure longer than a year, or at most two, in the garden's punishing conditions. The only willing variety with a personality at least close to that desired butterfly ebullience is the trailing Solomon Island ivy (*Epipremnum aureum*), with its two- to four-inch, bright green, yellow-maculated leaves of heart shape, which most of us from north of the tropics know as pothos, one of the most common houseplants. I use it as edging in the patio garden, as a low sprawler that helps conceal the massive amount of red crockery on the floor in a two-hundred-plant container garden.

Among other edging plants, annually replaced or retired in favor of still others, I have used the ferns *Nephrolepis philippinense* and *Adiantum aethopicum,* the purple velvet plant (*Gynura aurantiaca*), and the golden candle (*Pachystachys lutea*). Hello and goodbye. But my audience of Filipino and foreign tourists is so refreshed by the garden when it is newly supplied with these plants that the trouble and the expense of the annual touching-up seems well worth-while, in the human equation. How do I know the people are refreshed by what they see? What are the signs? They bend over and stroke the tips of the leaves of plants as if they were a cute dog's ears. They linger and study. They ask questions and take pictures. All very gratifying to the theatrical producer's instincts of this gardener.

So I figure I'm getting good value out of the bright but temporary edging plants. These, by the way, don't cost a lot, about half a U.S. dollar apiece, red clay pot and all, for plants of about a fifteen-inch spread. When they first begin to look tired, well before the last-legs-and-leaves appearance that would surely follow, I take the plants out of the garden and leave them in back of the building beside the parking lot. Somebody will grab them there, take them home, and nurse them back to health, and leave me feeling rather virtuous instead of seeming a heartless plant killer.

The numerous palms in the patio garden (mainly *Chrysolepis lutescens*) are more enduring. These remain lush for at least two years — unless attacked by the floral arrangers for the catered parties held frequently at Casa Manila. These fellows go to work like cutworms, cropping the fronds surreptitiously at night, while I'm away in my unwary bed. But this hasn't happened for almost a year now, owing to my finally having raised enough hell to be heeded.

A few varieties of the shrubs I've tried in the patio garden, a site difficult or even impossible for the health of plants, have actually prospered. The stalwart of stalwarts is

Dracaena surculosa, the vigorous wild form of this native of the forests of Mauritania, with dark green bamboolike leaves marked with light green spots. The wild shrub has about ten times the vigor and makes about four times the growth (to six feet high and thirty inches wide at top, from a slender base) of those dainty cultivated varieties *Dracaena surculosa* 'Kelleri' and 'Florida Beauty', with their showy white-spotted leaves, so well known to North Americans as indoor plants. The wild Mauritanian form grows as a loose fascicle of slender upright stems and lacy foliage. The plant really resembles no other species, yet suggests, in a dreamy way, a hybridization of nandina, cannabis, and bamboo. I've never seen this plant in any home, green-house, or plant shop anywhere in the world outside the Philippines, but it certainly deserves worldwide use as one of the most graceful of indoor furnishing plants, and one with the toughest of constitutions. It is the only plant in my patio garden with enough gladness to come into flower (those flowers I bring in from White Plains are another consideration). *Dracaena surculosa's* flowers are merely little white spiders of inflorescence, but so welcome they equal gardenias in my review of flowers I've grown.

Filipinos know and value this shrub for its willingness to tough it out in circumstances even more severe than in my garden. *Dracaena surculosa* is much used in pot-plant lineups on sidewalks outside such establishments as money changers', haberdashers', and honky-tonks along Mabini and Pilar streets, Manila's Sodom and Gomorrah. Through these two turbid sloughs of traffic everybody passes, nuns and the less holy. The clay pots that hold the dracaenas' roots often get broken, and there the plants will stand pot-less for months, with a base of exposed roots and hard dry soil, like blocks of brain coral. I pass by daily, on foot usually, and suffer for a moment, mentally sharing each plant's ordeal. I think about bringing a canteen of water with me next day to give the tortured dracaena a drink. So far my compassion has gone no further than thought; had I the aplomb to act it out, I can well imagine the circle of onlookers on the populous street, where the slightest out-of-the-ordinary event — the changing of a tire, the public tying of a shoe — will draw a stock-still audience. So the poor devil of a *Dracaena surculosa* suffers on.

The plant that, in my garden and on Manila's streets, ranks a close second in endurance of inner-city drought, bad air, and dark locations is another of the same genus, *Dracaena fragrans* — "fortune plant," to English-speaking Filipinos who pause in my garden to discuss the land-scaping. The common name may derive from the plant's wonderful propensity to parlay itself higher and higher, up from the meagerest foundation of soil and pot, a metaphor for easy money.

The species is West African in origin, and as with the Mauritanian dracaena, it is the wild form that is the more determined grower, far outdoing the cultivated varieties. Wild *Dracaena fragrans* bears only slightly lighter interior striping on its dark green, corn-plant–like leaves — much subtler leaves than those of the yellow-striped forms so abundant in the living rooms of the temperate world. The plainer *Dracaena fragrans* is at heart a green giant. Plants in fourteen-inch pots, which stood as tall as men, women, and children when I placed them in the garden in 1984, had attained heights of up to eleven feet by the end of the decade, and also a top-heaviness that now bowls them over in the occasional typhoon.

"Fragrans" stands for fragrant flowers, of which there are none where I grow the plant, and none that I've ever seen in many years of lookout in Manila and on Luzon, at varying elevations, in supposedly flower-inducing sunshine. I conclude that *Dracaena fragrans* is not free-flowering, at least not in the Philippines. But as greenery it is about as giving as a gardener could want, and probably more than enough in an apartment with an eight-foot ceiling. (Sawed off at a more practical height of stem, and given faith and regular watering during the weeks afterward, the dracaena will eventually stump-sprout and rise again.)

Two other shrubs are winners of merit badges for heroic self-reliance and achievement in the severity test garden I keep at Casa Manila. One is *Leea coccinea*, a lacy dark-bronze plant with much of the airiness of aspect and tiered branching habit of nandina. The other is parsley panax, *Polyscias fruticosa*, with finer lacy leaves than the *Leea*, of a light green. I have a special fondness for it, as a souvenir of my travels to the far island of Samar in the Philippines. Parsley panax grows there as a naturalized wilding in the scrub that accumulates within old coconut plantations. I collected seedlings of the plants years ago and added them to my pot garden, where they have got bigger and better-looking every year. Allow me the banal sort of pride that goes with such bring-'em-back-alive adventures. What gardener (who knows you well enough to confess ecological transgression) will not stop to show you, as I do now, the plant he or she espied in some far wilderness, dug up, brought home, and acclimatized? Intrepid gardener! Plant beyond price!

The arranging of some two hundred plants on the petro china of the patio unnerved me when the time first came to set them out. The old-time Spaniards might have had only a dozen plants in this space. I was concerned about violating historic style, considering that Casa Manila is supposed to be a faithful re-creation of Spanish colonial design. The small gardens of Spanish Intramuros — some of which show up, incidentally, toward the edges of street views and portraits of buildings in old photographs of the walled city — were careful reserves of precious open space, with most of the ground grassed or paved; trees and shrubs were few, formally positioned, and usually geometrically pruned; the little flower beds resembled petit fours, cookie-cut into the lawn, with the flowers as an icing of elaborate pattern. Mankind commands in such a garden; nature obeys.

After some thought sessions, I simply threw all that out and followed my instincts as a naturalist and plantsman, that is, to revel in botany like an anthropoid in the branches. My only theoretical excuse for an informal garden was that the patio setting seemed static enough already, and a formal arrangement of plants here could not amount to a garden with any spark of life in it.

As a plantsman, I have brought in as many kinds of as many shapes and sizes as I have thought I could balance in composing them all. I've attempted to give the congeries order and ease by a rhythmic arrangement of plant heights, of differing foliages, and of colors — the basic sensibility of an asymmetrically balanced garden.

To my eyes, the results look pretty good (and always in need of bettering). But since I am a tenant in this nationally important building, visited by thousands of Filipinos and foreigners, the audience must decide whether I have done right or wrong by the space. Visitors' responses, as I've written, have been rewarding. Those who, in walking through the garden, focus on the vegetation seem intrigued to discover a garden of lush tropicality in colonial surroundings. As for the Filipino visitors, I like to think that this race, known from archaeological findings to have lived amid the vivid greenery of these islands for thousands of years before the Spaniards came along with their rigidifying culture, responds to an earlier, more deeply felt appreciation of plants in easy community.

Would I have dared garden here at all if, before I placed the first plant, I had not felt certain the completed work would win an approving audience? Never in a lifetime. The garden is my theater, which I count on to bring me together with plants and people, the two life forms I most need and am forever trying to blend.

5

The Santo Kulago Garden

STAY FOR AN adventure story: the making of a home garden far, far from the city and the suburb. While the making of any home garden is an adventure like no other, the more civilized the setting, usually the more gently adventurous the episode, and the more primitive the location, the more heightened the drama. Mercedes, a well-water and Colman-lantern community on the island of Samar, some 450 miles southeast of Manila, is far enough away from it all to provide the adventure of gardening with certain dramatic touches. The story of my garden here requires a prologue.

I had come for the Santo Kulago (San´-toe Koo-log´-go), the Owl Saint, an early sixteenth-century carving, and while here I designed and installed a garden from scratch in excitingly swift time. The garden was a gift for the friends with whom I sojourned, and for me a diversion from my prolonged negotiations with the custodians of the Kulago, which I wanted (more than the poker player in me would have them know) for a museum display of pagan carvings. For several years now, my most satisfying work as an antiquarian in the Philippines has been the curatorship of old carvings within this country, keeping them here for the country's future — believing in a more stable time to come. Any culturally significant object that comes into my hands is not for sale but for display and eventual donation. Collections I have assembled are on display in Manila's Museum of Ethnology.

The eerie Santo Kulago fits reasonably into the tribal context of my current assemblage, although it is only half pagan; its other ethnicity is Christian. This hybrid icon furthers a notion I have that pagan religion in parts of the pre-Hispanic Philippines centered on an owl deity. As far as I know, nothing is recorded about this. But related evidence exists in certain northern Luzon idols with owl faces on otherwise human figures.

The Santo Kulago of Guiuan stands four feet tall, a carving of local hardwood blackened and eroded by nearly five hundred years of being stroked for luck by believers in its powers. The statuette has the talons, wings, stout body, and bluntly feathered tail of an owl; the head, rubbed nearly smooth, is still discernible as that of the Mother of Christ, crowned with a cross. Had the Spanish padres in earlier centuries ever learned of the existence of such an object, doubtless to them blasphemous in a monstrous degree, the Inquisitorial consequences of the discovery might still blister the imagination. But the Santo Kulago escaped detection — and survives, barely.

Belief in its beneficence is declining, replaced by fear

of a perceived malignity. Several decades ago, two children died in a household where the Kulago was kept. People here have very little modern medicine and did not understand the deaths, but supposed them to have been caused by the Owl Saint as punishment for its confinement indoors. In the years since the tragedies, this fragile object of wood has been kept outside in all weather. But now its custodians (lay priests of a sort) are at long last prepared to let go this centerpiece of their cult. They are fearful of selling, but are willing to bargain an exchange for a nice safe Santo Niño (a carving of the Christ Child), along with a shrine in which to house the Christian statuette and a celebration ("We always have dancing") to mark the passing of the Santo Kulago to a new custodian. That will be me, if all goes well in our ongoing negotiations.

One of my ambitions in this project is to take a picture of the Santo Kulago in the garden I've designed and planted in her name — perched there for an unforgettable moment like one of those terrific gargoyles in Italian Renaissance gardens, my counterattack against all the cute garden gnomes of the modern world. Then I will cushion and crate the Bird Lady for a boat trip to Manila, a voyage this claustrophobic icon will not like. Yes, I too have absorbed a few curies of the superstition that emanates like gamma rays from the Santo Kulago.

The landscaping of the namesake garden entailed the most fevered excitement I've ever known as a gardener. In a span of only nine days, we — half a dozen hired hands and I — completed a sizable layout. Two of my gardeners were relatives of Simon, my host. The other men were semistrangers known by sight but little more, who had shown up at the door asking for work once word about the project got around (in a flash).

I put no design on paper. Rather, I used something of the physicality of Leonard Bernstein, molding music with his bare hands and every joint, in outlining in the air and on the ground the garden shapes I had in mind. Verbal communication was much handicapped, since all the hired help except one man spoke only rudimentary English and I possessed almost nothing of their Visayan dialect. My single communicant understood some hundreds of words of English, and additionally proved the most self-reliant of the workers. I appointed him foreman.

The garden we made covers only seventy by seventy feet of ground, but is large in the sense that it is a complex composition entirely handmade, with the chopping and digging away of weed trees (acacia) and brush, with extensive regrading, with the laying out of walks and paths, and with generous planting, always characteristic of my work. We went on many a search for plants in the wild, and also in the tropically joyful little patches of private garden in front of houses in nearby Guiuan. There are no nurseries in this remote backwater, but we found people rather poignantly ready, in a community where cash is hard to come by, to sell plants from their gardens. Guiuan is a perpetual village, whose population has reached the small-city proportions of some twenty thousand — if one takes in the several thousand who live in the outlying district, Mercedes, where I was guest and gardener.

We are here in one of the poorest of provinces in a poor nation. Nobody is starving, but need makes nearly everyone eager, and a majority somehow light-hearted. I'm going to be dangerously honest in saying that it is a thrill to come to such a place, to get away from the more egalitarian democracies for a while and into the welcoming party a destitute society always makes for the relatively well-off. The welcome is devilishly attractive to many footloose individuals, of which I am one; to corporations of all sizes; to cults and religions; even to nations. Some arrive shining-faced to offer faith, hope, and charity; others arrive hard-eyed and hellbent on the crassest of exploitation; but the more usual comer blends into a devious subtlety any of these reasons for being in the Third World.

Mercedes lies several miles outside Guiuan, at the point where houses thin out to hundreds of feet apart beneath the coconut trees. In one of the houses lives a family I've known for many years. The grandfather, Simon, is mayor of Mercedes. In years past I had visited the family several times, the last trip seven years before this writing. In the interim there were only three other visits by foreigners to Guiuan and Mercedes.

A bearded backpacker came, to sit alone on the coral-and-shell sand well out of town and gaze at the surf, musing, he said, or something like. My mayor friend tells me that after he asked the young man a few municipal questions and got straight answers, nobody bothered him while he sat there three or four days, after which he moved on.

Then an international team of medical botanists (two women and four men of Filipino, American, Japanese, German, and Australian nationality) came to Mercedes and spent a month with the mayor and his family. The visitors sacked out at night on the dirt floor of the lower story of my friends' house, cooked their own morning and evening meals on Primus stoves, and spent their days walking the many miles of footpaths hereabouts or making day trips farther abroad in eastern Samar, collecting plant specimens and gathering data on folk medicine from the farm and fisher families.

The third foreign party to arrive, a retired G.I. (so he introduced himself to the mayor), stayed and married. He is the town's only foreign resident, aside from my occasional self. A voluble talker, the American pops into the mayor's office frequently. He says he likes it here because the living is easy. He goes to the weekend gamecock fights along with most of the rest of the male population. Simon asked if I would have a word with him about this. Seems that the fellow gets exercised and loudly profane in the hugger-mugger of the gambling, the flying feathers and blood, enough so that the piously conservative *provincianos* are put off by his sidelines performance.

But I never spoke with the American. We drove past him, my gardeners and I, while he was walking along the road and we were going the opposite way on a sortie for plants. I called out a friendly hello and got back stony silence and a look of horrification — of a total primordial hominid, aghast, I would say, over encountering a probably dangerous stranger in his territory. He had obviously not yet heard I was around, could have recognized my nationality from the single word I spoke, and seemed to prefer never coming face to face with another American. Simon conjectures that the man may be on the lam, as are so many Americans in the Philippines, but considers him harmless enough, except for language. To me he seems to fit precisely the description of that old-fashioned Pacific habitué the beachcomber. I'll leave him to it. Plant-gathering is my game here.

But earthwork would come first. I mentioned that the visiting medical botanists had sacked out on the dirt floor of the house. So I had always thought it to be — hard-packed red earth, and so I still think of it. Actually, it is not. I investigated with a penknife, having certain doubts, and found that the floor is concrete, permanently coated with tracked-in, ground-in red earth. Sweep it, sluice it, it still comes out a floor of red dirt.

The ruddy floor was the irritant that goaded me into starting the garden, or at first the earthwork part of the landscaping. Why keep on, until the end of time, tracking in mud in wet weather, dust in dry? I would build a clean walkway leading from the road to the house and do away with the old earthen path. I had the time — my previous visits had been too brief to scheme up such a project.

First I took a poll. I asked eight or nine members of a household of eleven permanent residents whether they would rather track in dirt or sand, having in mind a walk topped with beach sand. Unanimously, the family members opted for the sand. They may have been more tired than they had realized of living with an earthy floor, or possibly they were just being agreeable toward my proposed change. (Why did I not add cement to the path sand, fixing it into place as concrete? Good question. Ecclesiastic answer: Concrete would have been against my greenie religion, a sacrilege in this woodsy garden surrounding. I could no more bring myself to spread concrete in these circumstances than Greenpeace could sell whale oil.)

Work began with the six-inch-deep excavation of a walkway. We then neatly bordered the sides of the excavation with small squarish limestone rocks, hammered into the ground to the soil level outside the walk, as architectural a piece of work as could be made with natural stone, my idea being to strike a balance between Nature and man. The remainder of the excavation we nearly filled with limestone rubble tamped down to a reasonable smoothness. (When available, crushed oyster shells can be used to make a similar naturalistic walk suiting a coastal property.) A top dressing of white beach sand finished the job.

The walk looked good, but as anticipated, a little of the sand did find its way into the house, all the way up to the second-story floor of hardwood. In time, I expect the problem will largely correct itself as the sand sifts down into the crevices of the limestone rubble, leaving a smooth, firm surface. For now, as in years past, two or three teenage girls in the family are on sweep-and-polish detail first

88

thing every morning. The light scattering of sand will be, I think, no more problem for them than the eternal red earth. The girls sweep up with besoms made of the stiff midribs of coconut fronds. Then, *reesh, reesh, reesh*: for a quarter-hour this abrading sound continues, while the girls rub the downturned halves of dry, fibrous coconut husks back and forth across the floor with bare feet. It is the universal floor-polishing technique of this nation. *Reesh, reesh* is the sound of a steady home life, and of determination to put on a civilized polish.

The abrasive music wakes me up and calls me to duty, the determined landscaper, a polisher of Nature. Work on the walk got my mind going on a visualization of the whole front yard as a garden, instead of the jungly tangle it was. The most imaginative of mental pictures was not mine, however, but that of Simon, now my newfound garden friend. We were standing at the roadside end of the grand walkway — wide enough for two people to walk abreast — that now replaced the immemorial dirt path. Clumsily, I remarked that the new walk seemed to me a better approach to a mayor's house. He replied with his usual modesty, that theirs was only a simple life and his a simple mayorship.

For a moment I feared I might have been intrusive with my project, and patronizing with my careless remark, but then I felt gloriously redeemed with his next words. Evidently he was more pleased than he let on with the walk of sand, for he suggested that I extend the sand all along the road front of the property (about 150 feet). The ground here was sloped, so the sand would be not for the walking but for the looking. I was intrigued with the idea — I'm always fascinated with garden follies, anything of fine use-lessness, from topiary to Japanese sand mounds — and I went right ahead and had the white sand laid in a neat swath, separating road and roadside grass from the garden. We spread our tropical snow tidily, several feet wide, a foot deep, formally sloped and patted smooth at the sides. Aesthetic evaluation: rather good, less than great. The tall roadside grass detracted from the composition, as did the roadway itself.

I've noted that much of the calming effect of shaped sand in the Zen gardens of Japan depends on a richness of solitude supplied to the sand by a surround of greenery or, in the case of Ryoanji, by a stucco wall, with a mysterious, inchoate landscape fresco imparted by water stains. I decided that our sand ribbon was too stark on its own and needed interrupting with plants here and there.

What to grow in pure, salty sand? Spider lily (*Crinum asiaticum*), a Samar native that grows abundantly on sea-shore sand drifts nearby, as it does on many another Asian Pacific shore, and also on those of Florida, the Gulf states, and southern California. The species is a sumptuous foliage plant, with evergreen sword leaves in a stalked rosette rather too big to put one's arms around entirely, and a large white liliaceous flower, ribbon-thin in its petals and other parts. We made a sortie to the beach for spider lilies and found them easy to dig, easy to transplant. Clusters of

90

the colossal leaf rosettes judiciously spaced along our sand berm made all the difference.

Correction: not quite all. There was still the lank roadside grass — and no means of cutting it, no garden tools for sale anywhere in Guiuan. The single home-gardening tool most local people use is the machete, for chopping down trees, brush-slashing, weeding, tilling, planting, and harvesting. The local grass-tidying tools are water buffalo and goats. I might have brought in the latter appetite, but suspected that a goat would probably make short work of the spider lilies, and would surely trample the carefully shaped sand.

The nearest store selling garden tools was in Tacloban, an overnight boat trip away. We sent Yuling, a son-in-law of Simon's, who knows his way around the city. I drew a sketch for him of the garden tool we needed — hedge loppers. I'd seen them used in Manila, as the best hand tools for barbering patches of grass.

Yuling was glad to have the couple days' work involved in the journey, and I was hugely grateful not to make the trip. For him it would be a routine run that he could sleep through, as I've seen in making the crossing with him in times past, envying his tough ease in a situation that for me is hard going. Gangplank and decks treacherous with grease. Hundreds of people crowded onto three decks. Cattle fitted in with humanity on the lowest level. Canvas cots so close together the frames touch. No other facilities, no amenities or services. Gigantic tropical *cucarachas* cruising around like toy cars. The pitch and roll of a small boat on a dark sea. Unreal as a ghost, as my own doppelgänger, I arise from my cot and look all around in the dim deck light. Everyone else is asleep, absolutely everyone. I am alone in the world except for a hidden figure in the wheelhouse, steering the vessel. It is Charon, and this is a voyage of doom.

Eight times over the years I have made this night crossing, in four round trips going to Guiuan to visit Simon and family, then back toward Manila. There is no other way for me. There could be, in a more settled time. Bus service is available between Guiuan and Manila, with an inter-island crossing by bridge, but part of the route is through bandit country, where buses are occasionally held up, and much of the island of Samar along the way to Guiuan is controlled by insurgents. Simon and others have advised me not to take the bus.

While waiting the two days for the hedge loppers (for which I had other plans beside the neatening of the roadside grass), the rest of us cleared the front yard of invading banana plants, chance seedlings of coconuts, and bullwhip vines that had lashed around everything else. The workers uncovered splendid limestone boulders, taller than men, hidden beneath vines and fallen coconut fronds as secretly as Cambodian sculptures drowned in verdure. There was that archaeological resemblance, but in form and geological species the stones were similar to the Taihu rocks of classical Chinese gardens, their shapes a seeming paleontology of enormous vertebra, pelvic saddle, cranial ridge, and less identifiable excrescences of bone, all protruding from a stony matrix. The osseous cups and tunnels of these water-sculpted rocks would be perfect containers for whatever perching plants we could find in the wild.

A mile away, on a moonish face of almost untraversably rough limestone, grew ancient trees twisting forth from crevices. Saddles in the tree branches supported orchids, ferns, and other epiphytes. I took a few of each, not without the misgivings of an informed friend of the biosphere. Fortunately for the well-being of the island's weave of wildlife, my theft was of a rare order, and the plants common. Very few local gardeners have considered any native plant worth transplanting into their home gardens. Only exotics are generally accepted as ornamental. Of course, from my viewpoint as a visitor from overseas, the indigenous plants were the most marvelous of exotica.

We brought them home in our trusty tricycle, our everyday transportation and carryall. A tricycle in Filipino parlance is a motorcycle with a sizable enclosed sidecar containing little welded perches, for the squeezing in of as many as eight passengers. The tricycle is the main means of transportation on the island. I used one whose owner-driver was Gonzalo, a friend of the family, full-time during the making of the garden.

On another of our many botanical forays into the wilds, we discovered a local rarity, a single plant, which I felt perfectly at ease collecting. It grew in the shelter of coconut palms, in mellow, settled sand peppered with humus, a few hundred feet inland from the seashore. I'm sure I saved it by collecting it, for I was told that pigs wandering from farmyards relished the tuber of the species. The lone specimen we found had somehow been overlooked, but it would be only a matter of time.

This plant is a magnificent green creature, a seven-foot-tall, stalked perennial with an umbrella of segmented leaves three feet across, of a tender spring green, as we of the north would say. Surmounting the leaves, capping the plant, is a large daddy-longlegs inflorescence of little green flowers in an open head, accompanied by tan filaments draping down nearly a foot, dancing in any current of air. In all, a plant gentle and friendly, yet imposing and strange.

With machetes, the men dug the giant easily from the sand, which sifted away, exposing its tuber and roots. Yet this huge perennial, lettucy tender of leaf, sustained no shock on the trip home. Transplanted, it stood there in the garden's blazing afternoon sun, and to my astonishment did not wilt but waited serenely for the coming of the rain. The month was December, in the midst of the rainy season; later that same afternoon, the sky roiled and hard rain fell.

The gardener can get away with almost any rough uprooting and planting at this time. Everything we planted has lived, rooted down, and resumed growth. The rain falls unfailingly, savingly, at some time during each sunny day and again during the night. Plants in this climate function as growth bombs, compacted in their cells and chemistry during the dry season. The coming of the rain triggers the cartridge plant into an explosion. It has no

94

program for falling back now, only for outing. The death of greenery seems impossible at this season.

At night, with the tropical downpour striking the tin roof of the house as fiercely as a dump truck load of ball bearings, I rejoice with the garden. I picture each of its plants drinking up. That great leafy parasol I saved from the pigs comes to mind especially. If it were ever exported, to stand in a palm house at Kew or at Longwood Gardens (for in Samar the plant grows beneath palms), gardeners might make pilgrimages to see it in bloom. What is its Latin name and family membership? Where else do its generic relatives, if any, live in the world? For answers, I must consult the botanists at Manila's Santo Tomás University. For the present, I'll call the plant — what? Something to show empathy with its struggle for existence in a pig's world. I'll call it Snout-Me-Not.

The native name is a lengthy run, too difficult for me to learn by ear. The name of any native plant, however small and seemingly obscure, that I have asked after has instantly been given to me in the Visayan language, and instantly lost. The ethnobotany of Samar remains fresh in the minds and usage of the locals. Snout-Me-Not's starchy tuber is employed to stiffen Sunday-best clothing. The plant is still common enough to harvest in areas where pigs do not roam.

Belly-up Vine is my provisional name for another superbly suitable garden plant that we brought home from the woods: a moderate climber with handsome dark glossy leaves widely spaced on its whippy branches — big leaves, the shape and color of those of Canary Island ivy; but the Samar Island plant cannot be of the ivy genus, or at all related. It bears clusters of showy berries, white at first and quite like fruiting mistletoe; later the berries turn red. The men use these berries in the manner that Amazonian Indians use the rotenone-producing Derris vine (could my plant be related?), as a poison to be steeped in streams to paralyze fish, which are then gathered for food as they float belly up.

In Samar, a keen appetite for wild foods — any catchable and chewable sea creature, bird, or small animal, wild greens, and, the prize of all, honey — undoubtedly assists the general good health of a people whose staple diet is fish, rice, starchy cooking bananas, and starchy root vegetables. Raiding the stores of the wild bees is considered the most macho of all foraging. The sport came home to me when my workmen, clearing the rank vegetation from the boulders in the garden site, discovered a bees' nest, a buzzing citadel in a culvertlike hollow within the rock at soil level. Work stopped while all hands gathered around to discuss an attack on the bees. Several of the men shoveled away dirt, then the bravest of them borrowed a shirt from the back of a coworker (or, in the atavism of the moment, a fellow tribesman), wrapped it around his own arm and hand, and plunged up to his shoulder into the hole leading to the nest. The bees milled furiously around him. He must have received stings, but gave no sign. He brought out a disc of honeycomb and handed it to the shirtless one. Time and again he plunged in for more discs and handed them around, including one for me. The rounds of honey-comb held mostly wiggling bee grubs, with only a few of the cells filled with honey. I bit carefully, avoiding the frantic jelly babies. It is the sensible custom here to de-vour honeycomb entirely, grubs, wax, and honey. But the wigglers are one of the few native dishes I find unmanage-able. I'm a pretty good food tourist, and have tried such Philippine delicacies as locusts boiled in oil (once will do it for me), the huge monitor lizards of Samar (tough as tires), even stewed dog with gravy (flavorful, and a fine dish of revenge considering the long insult I have endured from dogs that trot into my gardens and do not entirely leave).

On gustatory occasions such as these I find myself to be George amid the alien corn. Inwardly, I ask these honey-raiders, who have shared the loot with me, whose rich culture I can only sample while standing on the fringe, Do you read me, gentlemen? Do you see a garden taking shape? Can you accept the old plants in this new use? Would that I could communicate to you my keen aware-ness of our employing certain of the island's indigenous plants solely for their form rather than for their utilitarian value, perhaps for the first time in the many-millennia hu-man history of the region. It turns out I'm the natural heir of the region's ethnobotany, as the pleasure gardener is everywhere the heir of the forager and farmer.

Day six. Our work here with soil, sand, rocks, and plants is coming together in a free-form design, which fea-tures, in place of a central lawn, a broad, rather oval sea of white sand spread over a swale of low ground shaded by coconut palms. Turf steps and grass paths connect the sanded area with beds of ground covers and flowers on an upper level in sun. The men dug some thirty cubic yards of loam from a distant part of the property and carried it to the garden site on litters, in order to make an easy grade between the upper and lower garden areas.

The grass in the garden, planted out as sods, has historical import in addition to handiness as instant lawn. We brought the grass, of the Bermuda species, home from a lawn planting that dates from the Second World War. It still grows in the vicinity of an American army hospital and barracks, a complex entirely gone except for concrete roadways, now healed over in many places by a neat carpet of this finely textured, low-growing turf. My men peeled it off with machetes — suspicious activity to water buffaloes grazing close by. The dark, humorless beasts raised their heads and with their eyes asked for an explanation.

In our garden, carpets of transplanted Bermuda grass lead between the tall Taihu rocks — hanging gardens now, their crevices cloaked with native ferns and orchids, and also with an exotic from Mexico, *Russelia equisetiformis*. I feel sure the Spaniards brought the plant, as they did so many hundreds of others, in the centuries of the galleon trade between Acapulco and Manila. I've not seen the *Russelia* in the Mexican wilderness, but would guess it to be a natural cliff-hanger. It loves rock faces (or hanging baskets), from whence it cascades in a mass of slim, equisetum-like, broomy branches and scarlet tubular flowers, a brilliant show throughout summer. The plant has become a garden favorite in the world's warmer regions, including the southwestern United States.

The garden's old-new Bermuda grass leads on to free-form beds of ground covers — the native oak-leaf fern (*Drynaria quercifolia*), a perfectly willing terrestrial as well as a natural epiphyte; a starry white little Samar woodland flower, like a much larger *Trientalis*, yet still a miniature; rosy amaryllis and silvery green leaf clumps of lemon grass (*Cymbopogon citratus*), obtained from a neighbor who lives a few minutes away along a trail; white daisy chrysanthemums (*C. morifolium*) and bronze-dark coleus of a sturdy, stem-rooting variety, two of the perennials we obtained from gardeners in the village.

Our tricycle trips to Guiuan in search of cultivated ornamentals became the talk of the town. There are no nurseries here, in lieu of which we embarked on a series of politely acquisitive visits to private gardens, Gonzalo in the driver's saddle, Pachito and Berting, Simon's sons, joining me on perches in the cab. We drove along streets lined with little gardens lush with the same kinds of colorful shrubbery that one finds throughout the tropical garden world. Commonest of all were the hibiscus and crotons, the latter in dozens of leaf forms, most of them splashed with warpaint colors, red, yellow, or white on green, but in rare instances plain green and peaceable.

Here in one garden is a line of various crotons planted in sand, among them two shrubs of a light, bright green, and like a narrow oak leaf in foliar form. At the base of the crotons grow big clumps of maidenhair ferns (*Adiantum raddianum*). Berting, who is known in the neighborhood, knocks on the door of the little dwelling of paintless, weather-silvered boards. A woman, eightyish, answers, greeting him by name. He explains that we are planting a garden at his father's house. Could she possibly sell us a few of her plants? The reply: an emphatic yes. (I'm surmising from the nods, agreeable looks and tone, the word for word of the conversation, in a language I cannot actually follow.) The men dig one of the oak-leaved crotons, a five-foot-tall-and-wide specimen, from the loose sand of the garden. Every bit of root comes up with the shrub: a sure winner. The men ball and burlap the root mass, using for burlap the leaves of a back-yard banana and for string tough strips of the same leaf. Into the tricycle cab with the croton; five bushel-size clumps of maidenhair fern follow. Where will I sit? Can't be done. Berting and I wait while the others drive home with the load and return. Berting proffers payment for the plants, and for an instant before accepting, the grandmotherly gardener instinctively places her hands in a steeple position of prayer, as if confronting amazing grace. I have a feeling she has not held any money of her own for a long time.

For the rest of the day and all the next, we knocked on doors at little gardeny places. Berting's polite requests for plants were never refused, in this community where annual earnings, translated into American currency, average two hundred dollars. That is not per capita income, but actual pay for a year's work. We were at least as welcome as money, and found friendly willingness in gardeners to part with duplicates of their best plants. I was never so rapacious as to ask for a prized one-and-only.

We gained about thirty kinds of cultivated plants for our garden (in addition to an equal number of wild plant species already gathered). In the kitchen garden at the back of one woman's house grew another of the great discoveries of this garden adventure, equal to Snout-Me-Not and Belly-up Vine. I call it the Tasty Bush. This food plant is a dainty shrub, apparently of the family Papilionaceae. It forms several slender trunks, fine branches, and roundish little leaves, pea green and astonishingly tender for leaves munched raw right off a woody shrub, as I did in a taste test. The flavor combines the fodderish freshness of short-cooked sugar pea pods with the savoriness of pinto beans properly simmered for hours. The plant would make a distinct addition to the repertory of the world's better-known vegetable flavors.

Asia is said to have thousands of varieties of vegetables that remain rare or unknown in the West, and I think their obscurity is due to the fact that they are in the main not world-beaters for flavor, the like of carrots, tomatoes, and onions. Tasty Bush is the exception. With the worldwide search now being conducted by the West for new flavors among fruits and vegetables, I would expect branchlets of Tasty Bush to appear in our supermarkets before very long — say, in the early 2000s.

This shrub not only tastes morish, it is useful landscape material. Our garden hostess had made hedges of it by sticking into the fertile sand of her waterfront garden line-ups of fifteen-inch or so lengths of branch. They rooted within a week, she explained, and the resulting hedges, kept at a height of four and a half feet, formed screens within which were secreted wellhead and chicken coop. Her landscape use of this narrow, upright shrub suggested to me another employment — as mural foliage, which was needed in our new garden: something that would serve as an informal espalier. We purchased three of the woman's five hedges, and while the men dug, she at once replanted, inserting cuttings of Tasty Bush wherever the established shrubs had been removed.

At home, we planted a close line of this comestible in an eighteen-inch-wide strip of ground between a side wall of the house and the new sidewalk, which happened to lead directly to the kitchen. That would be of help in keeping the plant espaliered, a necessity in the narrow bed in which we placed it. I'm thoroughly pleased with this planting — good eating, good-looking, with wood that is easy to cut and ready to branch out from stubs, properties crucial in any plant that is maintained as a hedge or living mural.

The hedge loppers had come in good time. We will use this tool to keep the mural planting tidy, and to trim the Bermuda and road-edge grasses as well. The overall main-tenance of the garden will provide chores enough to keep a man busy several hours a day. Take note of the use of the verb *provide,* as in *bestow.* An actual job is in germination. I asked my foreman to stay on as gardener, daily for a year's time. His name is Ray, his age nineteen or twenty; he is a quiet, well-mannered fellow, with jumpy bundles of muscle disharmonious with the personality. I first knew him when he was a small boy who never called himself Ray. "My name eez Reynaldo," he used to pipe with chesty cheer and self-determination. He was a bright-eyed lad who would proudly perform for us grown-ups, on request, recitations he learned at school. It is a thing children are asked to do here during company evenings at home. And "What is your ambition, Reynaldo?" All Filipino schoolchildren are supposed to have their ambition — their career plans — on the tip of their tongue. Whatever Reynaldo's ambition was, I've forgotten. And perhaps, overwhelmed by reality, Ray has as well.

Ray's eyes rounded with dumbfounderment when I told him that he had a regular job if he wanted it, for regular money. Afterward, he was overheard (and reported to me) describing his new job to Gonzalo and the garden help. Gonzalo asked wonderingly, "You mean to say you will have five hundred coming in *every* month?" Five hundred pesos at the current exchange rate is eighteen dollars (a salary set by Mayor Simon, the young man's uncle, to be sent by money order). With Ray, the newly graduated master gardener, I walked all around the 70-by-70 domain we had built when he was merely foreman. The work was as complete as I could make it, for the present. On our walk, I pointed out all the upkeep to be done during the next year, until my planned return — and recognized that I had been only partly understood. To anchor the instructions, I wrote them down on a sheet of paper. Still not enough. I had the family (several women members, good at English) translate and transcribe my briefing into the Visayan language. Here is approximately the message:

Keep the garden beds and the boulders weeded at all times. Cut back any plant that tends to overgrow another. (There's a point I could still teach myself.)

If the grass hasn't begun vigorous growth before the rainy season is over, give it water. Use your machete to edge the lawns and grass steps in the exact shapes we've made with the sods. Apply fresh sand to the sanded areas, as needed. Use the hedge loppers to keep the grass short, and also to keep the shrubbery at the side of the house flat against the wall. When the loppers are not in use, keep them wrapped in an oily rag. (Another admonition that I, a deplorably rusty gardener, could well take to heart.)

Time to get back on the dreaded boat for Taclobon, for a connecting flight to Manila. I was feeling MacArthurish about it — portentous and gloomy but resolute: I shall return. There is the unfinished business of the bird, and the garden, and friendship.

6

A Novice in
New Zealand

Mount Roskill, Auckland, New Zealand; December 25. We're going to have Christmas dinner here in a couple of hours, with guests arriving. Until then, until the utter last-minute need for me to arise from this chair and spruce up for dinner, I have some solid time left for jotting. The exercise is a good jog for the brain, I find, and tones up my conversational ability. I'll need some, well whetted. The men of this country practice a national style of roughhouse badinage, an exchange of verbal darts directed against your skin — gotcha! The women, of course, are more civilized — gotcha right back!

I've just arrived from Manila, on a flight to Auckland that I've made annually for some years now, one that never fails to bring on an attack of culture amazement (an agreeable form of culture shock). This trip is a bit like departing from a bordello and flying directly to a Sunday school picnic. New Zealand, pioneered in the nineteenth century by particularly able and no-nonsense Britons, remains recognizably what it was, a conservative farming community. The countryside, though much suburbanized, is still grassy green and open for miles; suburban streets seem startlingly clean and peopleless in their contrast to darkest Asia, which I've just left; the very air is a shock to the senses in its purity and quietness; and over all there is a palpable moral atmosphere, a kind of public pickle brine of rectitude.

Things are changing, of course. A couple of years ago, with much soul-searching and editorial bleeding, New Zealand's weekend blue laws were partly repealed. Now you can buy groceries on Saturday; on Sunday the stores are still shut tight as Tutankhamen's tomb. And *never* to be had is a bottle of beer or wine at a grocery store. Not yet.

This country, in the late twentieth century, reminds me in many nostalgic ways of the American farm town I grew up in during the 1930s. New Zealand is still a land where milk is delivered in bottles, and where it is generally safe to leave the money to pay for it in the empty bottle one places on the special little shelf in the mailbox stand. All is not Arcadian here, however. In recent years we Aucklanders have been stunned by the advent and rapid rise of big-city crime on downtown streets, mostly after dark when the nocturnal fauna come out. But the suburbs — Mount Roskill for one — remain as safe as any in the world, so I believe.

The first gardening I do when I arrive each year is visual. I go out and tour the garden, wandering and gazing. Each year I'm astonished at what I see in that first viewing. Are these the same plants I set out last autumn (April)?

Every fall, let me explain, I do much last-minute planting before I leave New Zealand, counting on autumn and winter rains to help root in and establish the new plants. The garden will grow on, now, through the mild North Island winter. I depart carrying clear mental pictures of shrubs and perennials in place within new compositions. When I see the plants again eight months later in the New Zealand sun, presto chango! Is it possible these are the same plants, so much bigger and handsomer? The sensation is that of seeing a suddenness of stems, leaves, and flowers, as in a time-lapse film. What a marvel is plant growth.

My other first impression of the garden leaves me aghast. The hedges are on the loose again. And I left them so trim and dignified last autumn. Plant growth, what a menace!

I mutter, but must admit that my annual chores of pruning are probably as restorative of trim frontage in myself as in the hedges. I spent a couple of bracing hours this morning hand-pruning the tapestry hedge — only twenty-one feet long, but nine feet high — which screens the house from the parking area (and from the western view out across the plains of suburbia). The pruning was my major contribution to our Christmas Day, since the hedge stands immediately in front of parkers, the first thing they see, and could not have been left shaggy on this occasion. Pruning the various native New Zealand shrubs that make up the tapesty hedge, plants I set out fourteen years ago, was easy for once, owing to my having come to Auckland earlier than I have for years. Got around to the pruning well in season this time, right at the turn of spring into summer, with the wood still in soft growth; the hardening of the wood, and its increasing resistance to pruning tools, begins with the coming of high summer. Tapestry hedge? Neither the term nor the garden device it stands for are, I think, in wide use around the world. I would like to come back to the topic later, with more leisure.

Following my major contribution to Christmas Day, my minor one is the bunch of Shasta daisies I picked in the garden, deleafed somewhat, and sheafed into a vase. The daisies now form the centerpiece on the dining room table, but will have to be removed and relocated to the mantle when the feast comes in and crowds the tabletop.

Eddying aromas of roasting lamb and turkey now fill the house. After my stint in the garden, I'm feeling as toothy as a tiger. Good old roast lamb, the eternal company dinner in this country of about 63 million sheep and 3 million people. The turkey is rather a novelty, though, a culinary Christmas card addressed to me and my Yankee heritage. What thoughtful friends I have in Auckland. Alicia and Bruce, Albert, Mo, and several children will be gathering here today. Some of these friends go back in my life to 1958, the result of meeting on an ocean voyage. We're gathering here at Mo's house, on the grounds of which, over the years, I've carried on most of my New Zealand gardening.

I must close now. It is time for me to start the great

cleanup, my metamorphosis from garden grub to an imago of neatness and urbanity.

※

December 26. It's all over except for leftovers and reminiscence. The Ghost of Christmas Past has been tugging at my sleeve today. It was at this season in 1976 when I first arrived at the house and lot on Auckland's Mount Roskill. A half-hour from the airport, well out toward the edge of a 15-mile-by-15-mile patchwork quilt of city, suburbs, and pastures, we drove down a long steep driveway and parked in front of a clapboard cottage painted an attractive tawny tan. We parked on a pad of concrete that almost completely covered the small front yard. Car, house, and we ourselves perched on a shelf of land bulldozed into a hillside. Indoors, we sat down for the national tonic, a cuppa (tea), following which I, feeling cabined after my long flight, asked my friends if they would mind if I went out on my own for a stretch and a look around the grounds. Go ahead, they encouraged; but there was really no garden to see, only what had come with the house when Mo had bought it a year before.

The tour was indeed not gardeny, rather a confrontation with concrete, scraps of lawn dried brown in drought, and tall frazzled weeds, including brambles. Most of the property fell away in a wooded ravine too steep to explore. Uphill, other cottages stared down from bare lots. The property offered a great saving grace, however, in a grand view — from the parking pad across the ravine's tree-tops — to the multimillion-dollar, parklike landscape of a golf course, and beyond to forested hills, bluish green in the distance. Well, let the view be the garden, I thought. For once I would keep my fingernails clean and spend my time on the beaches and the trails. As for the property on which I stood, I could see at a glance that this was a piece of land that would break the spirit and back. I would stay here awhile as a guest, and would renew old friendships. But I wouldn't touch the grounds.

Fat chance! Within a few days I had come around to being the irrepressible gardener. I began by conducting for myself an appreciation course in the property's better points — to the tune, if not the actual words, of the old song, "You've got to accentuate the positive, eliminate the negative." For the time being, at least, any liabilities could be dismissed.

On the plus side, the view. With only a little trick of supposing, the golf course transmuted into a manorial park; the visual sweep over hundreds of acres of lawn and trees, with a creek and a pond and no buildings in sight, became as good as the view from some Georgian or Edwardian hall in Britain, motherland of landscape parks. Probably better, in that my pretend parkland was free for the looking, with no terminal property taxes on it. People could stand here, dreaming on distances, and discover themselves to be as privileged, for the moment, as an Aberconway gazing from Bodnant across the greenscape to Snowdonia.

Poof! The scene dissolved to suburban Mount Roskill.

Any landscaping I undertook, such as the grading of soil and the adding of plants, should by design lead on visually to that grander world in view, merge with it, and so bring it all home.

On the plus side, still, the suburban lot was a generous one, several times larger than thousands of others on Mount Roskill. It totaled about three quarters of an acre, measuring all the ups and downs. The lot had "elevation," the landscaper's dream. The land was in fact precipitous. In platting (or plotting?) the dimensions of this property, the developers allowed it extra footage as compensation, since most of the land appeared worthless. Visualized in cross-section, the property formed a V: a ravine with the house perched on a serif of land at the top of one of two opposing slopes. Along their juncture, at the depth of the ravine, flowed a little creek almost totally concealed from where I stood, revealed fragmentarily between tree boughs in little mirror flashes of sun on water.

The sides of the ravine were about as steep as a child's play slide, which coincidence probably challenged the lad who lives within. I had to get down to explore the terrain beneath the shadowy tree canopy that filled the upper reaches of the ravine. Plunging downhill with legs and feet out of control, outmatched by the pull of gravity, I grabbed the trunks of trees (ponga, whiteywood, and red matepo, I would later learn) one after another in a zigzag way down, to keep from falling. I reached a tiny protruding lip of land near the bottom of the ravine, a level stopping place where the ground was clothed with an inviting forest grass. On hands and knees, I leaned out over the lip of earth and saw a blurred reflection of my face on the surface of the creek a few feet below. The same sight terrorized a school of tiny fish, which exploded away toward cover. I got up and stood quietly, captivated by the setting. Shafts of sunlight piercing through the overhead foliage warmed my shoulders. All was peaceful.

It was a perfect preamble for a visitation of some sort, and there was one. Two black-and-white birds no bigger than wrens materialized, flew toward me, hovered a little beyond arm's length, but did not settle. Constantly changing their places on twigs while spreading their long black-and-white tails into full fans, flashing them this way and that in a fan language probably as meaningful as that of flirtatious majas, the little birds looked me straight in the eye. Simultaneously, they blessed or cursed my presence with a song made of shrill cascading notes, piercing but pleasant, sounds such as a broken string of pearls might make bouncing down a marble stairway. I almost laughed aloud in my delight. This was my first encounter with New Zealand's fantail. In many meetings since, I have always regained a measure of my first pleasure in a little bird that flies up and studies you minutely while singing and semaphoring mightily. Yet I have never been able to decide whether the bird is fearlessly friendly or fearlessly cross in its message.

The main part of the ravine lay within the boundaries of my friend's property; its shallower end portions stretched across adjoining lots. Overall, its course was only about six

hundred feet long, and two hundred feet wide in its broad-
est central portion. Nevertheless, the wooded waterway
functioned as a nature reserve, supporting, besides fantails,
birdlife such as quick little white-eyes, shy thrushes, and
the big, bumptious tui (a melodious singer, though, in the
tenor register); there were those fingerling fish; cicadas,
among many insects and other small life; six kinds of trees,
and eight different varieties of native ferns. The full discovery of the latter would take about two years' time, for while
several of the species formed large, conspicuous colonies,
others were hidden away in twos and threes on the most
inaccessible steeps. And I would need a flashlight to guide
my way at night along the trails I would make in the ravine
to its deepest part, beyond the reach of moonlight, where
the most magnetic wildlife awaited, and awaits, just above
the flow of the stream, on a vertical black wall of earth: a
galaxy of glowworms, each a starry dot of silent white
light.

The ravine and the green view, then, amounted to two
property assets of rare order, by which the gardener might
connect with worlds pastoral and wooded. The opportunity
was all the more extraordinary for its situation in the midst
of suburbia, which rolled in from all directions except the
southern, the location of all that I've detailed with such
frankly childlike wonder.

❋

In that first, formulative year of my acquaintance with the
property, I thought out a plan for making the hillside lot

a more livable garden, and talked over my ideas with Mo and others of the family in an after-dinner discussion. I have now, all these years later, no record on paper of what I actually proposed that evening. Quite likely, I had not at the time thought of everything I list below, in an amalgamation of topics I surely touched on in our discussion and work actually done year by year. I would:

• Knock down and remove unsightly structures from the grounds — a tiny tin carport, iron corner-posted, badly rusted throughout; a chain-link and concrete post fence; a sagging board frame no longer supporting a passionfruit vine; a large laundry tree (or carousel, as some people call such contraptions) fixed in concrete in the back yard.

• Jettison the few sad, misplaced plants dating from the former owner's tenure.

• Grub out briers and gorse, pampas grass, kahili ginger, and other heavyweight weeds that infested the edges of the lot.

• Clean up the ravine. I didn't tell you, in my rhapsodizing over its nicer features, that the ravine had been used as a dump during the farming era that preceded the suburbanization of the neighborhood (during the mid-fifties to mid-sixties).

• Cut pathways throughout the steep property, to connect the shelf of land that held the house with a second shelf higher up on the hillside; and lay out additional pathways between the land shelves and the ravine, on down to the creek.

• Establish hedges for privacy and space division, making garden rooms of the open, starkly suburban front, back, and side yards of the house.

• Add foliage plants, and incidentally their flowers, in variety for visual entertainment, and to furnish a study garden of plants suited to the Mediterranean-type climate of Auckland, especially the New Zealand flora. (Note the primary consideration of foliages before flowers. But I probably kept silent about this in my presentation to my friends, virtual nongardeners, to whom flowers were almost the only idea. We were both naive. To this day, I am at work trying to establish a balance between foliages and flowers on a property that cries out for foliation — in a garden that also, I find, very much needs the freshening touch of flowers.)

• Reduce the sterile gray of concrete, so prevalent on the property, by placing plants that, in growing, would cover it over wherever possible and practical.

The items in the pitch I made that were most enthusiastically received were my offers to "jettison," "grub out," and "clean up." The "knock down" I suggested won approval more slowly, only after I sufficiently convinced my listeners that no garden, however fine, could stand up visually to junkyard uglies in its midst. Yes, I agreed, the rusting and sagging structures still had their uses and had not come free of cost, and yet. . . . Here I painted a picture of the garden as a bit of the earth entire, a visually unpolluted place for peaceful hours in privacy. The faces of my listeners relaxed into an approving peaceability. Had

I been a preacher, I might at this point have passed the plate. This was one of a few occasions in my life as a gardener when, on behalf of the garden, I have summoned up exhortatory powers I hardly realized I possessed. Lucky thing, all around, that I was born or early made a gardener and not a Mussolini.

I volunteered to do all the work myself, and in fact insisted on doing so, politely declining offers of help. I reckoned my friends were simply too busy with their careers to spare the time. Quite alone, and satisfied to be so, I myself would accomplish, in that first year and in years following, the cleanup and much of the rest I had outlined.

In short order I demolished three crummy structures that stood in the way: first, the little prefabricated carport, a corrugated tin roof supported by four posts of iron fancywork, the connecting bolts frozen with rust. It did not come down easily, but required a good one hundred blows with a sledgehammer, heavy work and an ungodly din. A neighbor in a house about four hundred feet away stood at her picture window, watching; and although we were too far apart for me really to see her face, I could sense in the hackled stiffness of her pose that we were, so to speak, not waltzing at all well together. I had true regrets about being, in her eyes and ears, a pain, however temporary. Would that I could always be an unobtrusive neighbor, but I have not always found that role compatible with being a creative gardener, a banger at times, then a dumper and spreader of fumy composts, and often a no doubt irritatingly active presence not far outside neighboring windows.

Patience, patience, I will plant plants between us. They will be friendlier than a fence, for they will be the right plants, maintained at a neighborly height. Behind kindly foliages, you and I will disappear from each other. All in good time.

Now I was ready to knock down the concrete post and chain-link fence at the far side of the parking pad. However, before I could take sledgehammer and hacksaw to this ghastly steel elephant-stopper out of a 1930s zoo, there were special New Zealand reasons for getting the neighbor on the other side of the fence (not the same one as the lady at the window) to agree to the demolition. Although the structure stood entirely within the property on which I was working, this nation has an established body of laws and quasilegal traditions concerning fences and hedges. The rules are active in contemporary suburbia, but date from an older, rural New Zealand, where they came about to protect vitally important pasture fencing and hedgerows. Once laid out, the fence or hedge took on a sacrosanctity quite apart from ownership by this or that neighbor. Both benefitted, therefore both were responsible for upkeep, and both had a say if the fence or hedge were ever to be taken down.

The word from the woman who lived on the other side of the fence was far happier than the body English I'd had from the lady at the window. The fence-side neighbor (who lived alone) agreed unhesitatingly that the fence could come down: She'd hated it from the start.

What do you know — a kindred spirit, a gardener

who placed the presentable higher than the mundanely practical. The fence did have practical value, at both sides. It would prevent a wayward car from rolling downhill onto the neighbor's neat little round of lawn bordered by rose-bushes. Eventually I placed several good-looking weath-ered boulders, each about the size and shape of a full-grown Galapagos tortoise, along the brow of the hill where the fence had been. The presence of stones of meaningful size in strategic places on one's property amazingly improves the accurate steering of cars, I find — true of my own driving as much as anybody's.

Next on my demolition agenda came the knock down and drag out of a crude scaffold of sagging boards, a meant-to-be vine support, from which the vine, an edible passion-fruit, had long since escaped and bounded upward among the branches of a native coprosma tree. I left it there, to its own climbing and clinging abilities. For about the next seven years (the remainder of the twenty-odd–year life span of this not long-lived vine) we harvested the hard-shelled fruit as it fell to the ground.

The fourth structure standing in the way of a garden stood and stood for a while, until I could figure out what to do with it. Couldn't outright kill this one; it had living value. It was the inevitable laundry tree. As with a ma-jority of New Zealand back yards, the one here was a shrine to this sacred tree and its votive pinnings. The central placement of the tree in the back yard was as usual; as usual, too, was the narrow concrete walk that led like a scar across the grass from the back of the house to the tree in its sanctum sanctorum. The most gardenable part of the property had been turned into a drying yard.

The steel tree species had undeniable purpose, as a place to hang the laundry; it had even taken on a kind of royal entitlement to the place. Who would dare change things, or bother to make a change? Need I pose the question? You know me. As I saw it, there could be no garden here until the laundry tree was out of the picture. Or, turn that around: There could be no picture here until the laundry tree was out of the garden, landscaping being none other than the making of scenery. Not only was the structure, with its steel scepter and nine-foot-wide wire crown, a visual tyrant in the setting, it was a physical obstacle, largely filling the narrow space. To walk on toward the undeveloped part of the property farther back, you had to bow and scrape to get past it. I did that once too often and decided: The time had come.

I took up a spade and started digging the tree out of the ground, with the idea of moving it farther off, to a decently obscure nook of fairly level ground I had found at some distance downhill on the property. This effort turned out to be one of the more memorable pieces of horse work I've ever undertaken in the name of gardening. The planter of the laundry tree had buried the lower part of its steel stem within a thirty-inch-wide, thirty-inch-deep concrete root ball, which weighed easily three hundred pounds.

After digging around the root ball, I used a nurseryman's technique for raising it out of the hole, by tipping the tree and root ball well over to one side, throwing a few

inches of dirt in the side of the hole exposed by the tipping, then tipping the tree back in the opposite direction;
more dirt; more tipping; until, little by little, I was able
to raise the concrete ball up to the level of the surrounding
soil. From time to time throughout this hour-long labor,
I was conscious of the jigging of curtains at the window of
one of the houses uphill. Behind the curtains stood a
woman who did not garden (she and her husband were
athletic, and were always running away from their property), a woman whom I'd seen in her yard only on those
twice-weekly occasions when she hung out the wash on her
own laundry tree. Now she stood covertly curtained, fascinated by my apparently lunatic performance. Unless one
is prepared to forgo the sympathies of one's neighbors
("He's a fair dinkum fellow"), one does not violate a laundry tree. There are probably ordinances, in this watchful
little country.

At last, having successfully hoisted the concrete ball, I
twirled ball and tree slowly, ever so carefully downhill,
straining to keep the dead weight of rounded concrete from
escaping my grasp and hurtling on to splash in the creek
at the bottom of the ravine. I eased the monster down to
the secluded niche I had found for it, some ninety feet from
the house. Here I replanted it, straight and serviceable,
and then planted a laundry garden (as we came to call it)
around the tree's steel stem. The composition included
lemon balm, balsam, and several varieties of mint, all in a
casual circle just outside the dripline of clothes hanging on
the tree; about the base of the stem I planted chamomile

as a wear-resistant ground cover. The taller herbs in the perimeter garden performed as a living potpourri, releasing a blended scent whenever the drying sheets and towels brushed against them.

For years the laundry tree remained in this distant, deliciously scented location. I made a point of hanging out the laundry myself whenever I was around, not minding at all the one-hundred-eighty-foot, downhill-uphill round trip. However, hausfraus besides myself chided me roundly; I remember especially a scolding by my old friend Alicia on my zany impracticality. (My best friends are my worst philistines.)

Then, in time, folding laundry trees came on the market in New Zealand, of the size and compactibility of big beach umbrellas. This new device seemed one I could tolerate in the back-door garden, knowing that its possession of this favorite garden room would last only for the few hours of each laundry session. I made a place for the newfangled tree very near where the old one had stood. To secure its base during use, I buried a sixteen-inch length of plastic pipe, big enough of bore to hold the tree stem vertically in the ground. Rocks tamped around the pipe keep the tree from woozing about in the ground when it is wet and soft. The tree has proved to work just fine. I'm really not much of a handyman, so I take a probably ridiculous amount of pride in contemplating it standing there sturdily at work. Then there is the bonus satisfaction of taking it down and regaining the garden.

The old, exiled monstrosity could now leave the property altogether. Mo came up with an idea both humane and humanitarian for getting rid of the thing, and telephoned a needy family (Mo is a social worker). Two men and a boy came out — muscular grown-ups with gardens of tattoos, all three with Rastafarian dreadlocks (the cult has its adherents here). They dug up the old laundry tree, tussled it up the hill, and trucked it away. Witnesses in this staid neighborhood must still be pondering the pageant as a part of the extraterrestrial mysteries.

❁

Having cleaned up the upper land shelves of the property to a gardenable condition, I addressed my janitorial efforts to the depths of the ravine, a pit of litter. My Augean task was similar, I believe, to that of almost every gardener who begins work on a country property where rustics have preceded one's residency. The story is certainly that of some of our more famous gardeners.

For a sympathetic word, for a literary arm around the shoulders, I reread Vita Sackville-West's account of beginning her garden at Sissinghurst Castle by dismantling and hauling away a gigantic midden containing within its mold an astonishing number of sardine tins; sardines would seem to have been central to the diet of the previous tenants. Even more applicable to my task was Margery Fish's classic *We Made a Garden,* in which she recounts having restored to its natural decency a creek gully chock-a-block with the more die-hard items of trash.

Now I too confronted a creek gully — or, as I prefer

to call it for the sake of felicity, a ravine — in an awful mess. For many years the ravine had routinely served the primitive human instinct, still operative, to get rid of dead bodies and other debris by tossing everything down the nearest bank. Indeed, I did turn up remnants of bodies — femurs and a scapula brown with age — half buried in leaf mold. These discoveries gave me a start, until I realized the bones were too big to be human, or to be of anything lesser than a farmer's ox.

Almost all the rest of a good ton of ejectamenta that I carried or rolled or dragged up the bank was the usual assortment of litter that provokes the gardener's ire. After all, with many of us coming to realize that Earth is everyone's house, we wait impatiently for the slower learners to become house-trained.

I had quite a time dragging out a car axle that had some leggy parts attached to it, a crocodilian of steel, burnt umber with rust. Had this thing lain rusting away for another fifty years, until it got some Henry Moore holes in it or a Giacometti crustiness of surface, it might have been worth keeping as found sculpture. I'm one of those gardeners intrigued by shapely pieces of old iron. There must be many of us, for I often see such iron on display, in the form of old farmyard or mining equipment or other rusting pieces of the regional past. It takes at least fifty years, though, for rust-art to evolve from trash, and the car axle I fell heir to hadn't sufficiently ripened. Away with it.

My archaeology with a rake turned up, in a ton of stuff, one small artifact worth saving, an early twentieth-century cream dipper handcrafted of German silver — not silver at all, but silvery, a farm kitchen implement identified for me by my friend Bruce. Bruce, who descends from New Zealand pioneers, remembers such cream dippers still being in use during his boyhood in the 1930s. It was a time when Aucklanders, cream dipper in hand, went out to the family milkshed, where the day's dairy yield cooled in large amphorae of the same nonsilver. Our discovered cream dipper, dented and discarded in the old days, is now on display on the kitchen windowsill.

Working the ground in my gardening these later years, I always keep a sharp eye out, in hope of turning up richer treasure — a giant moa bone or a Maori jade amulet. Here and everywhere in Auckland, the soil is pregnant with the past.

7

Learning,
Forgetting

WHEN THE TIME CAME to begin selecting plants for my New Zealand garden, I discovered that I was appallingly ignorant of the plant repertory of the region. Three decades of gardening in the cool, temperate Pacific Northwest, garden land of conifers, rhododendrons, Japanese cherries, and a thousand other winter-craving plants, counted for little in North Island, New Zealand. Here was more a Mediterranea of front-yard palms, bougainvillea, hibiscus, and several thousands of other frost-abhorrent plants. I became a garden freshman all over again. Garden centers became my classrooms, reference books on plants my required reading. I found two books to be invaluable in my studies, *Gardening with New Zealand Plants, Shrubs and Trees* (of which I will say more later), and the *Western Garden Book*. This latter volume, the main opus of the Sunset line of gardening books, is readily available in the salesrooms of Auckland's garden centers. It remains the world's only complete one-volume gardening guide that includes an encyclopedia of plants suited to all climates, from the subarctic to the uncertainly frost-free (the sub-tropical). The book slights only the tropical zones.

In my decades of gardening in the Pacific Northwest, I have literally read to pieces — cover sloughing off, pages giving up their glue and falling out — two successive copies of this endlessly informative, wretchedly bound book. Here in New Zealand, I'm on my third. Well, there are reasonable excuses for the cheap binding: The book is bargain-priced, and the company has periodically brought out expanded editions, just before one's old flaky copy is quite ready to be converted into garden mulch by being scattered on the compost heap. Pages to potash.

Along with my reading in the garden gospels, I visited garden chapels — neighborhood garden centers — all over town. I found much repetition in their offerings, but also plants special to each place of business. New Zealand's garden centers are patterned after the American invention of that name. In Auckland, how familiar was everything I found: platoons of plants standing in containers; rooting medium of sawdust or some other humus, with sand or not; usually no salesperson in sight, except for a kid watering plants at the moment, who wouldn't know a gerbera from a geranium anyway; grocery carts to hold one's prizes; a trundle to the cash register, a roll out to the car, and away. How well, in a thousand runs, have I come to know and appreciate the ritual. It is undeniably convenient, and reminds me only slightly of the automation episodes in Charlie Chaplin's *Modern Times*.

In my first six or seven visits to Auckland garden centers, I went strictly as a student, not as a buyer. I was thankful for the impersonality of the sales system, for it provided me with private moments in which to nip with a penknife — harmlessly enough, I convinced myself — a leafy twig from this or that attractive unknown plant. I would fold the specimen in a small sheet of paper on which I had written the plant's name, together with other information garnered from the label, such as the extent of the flowering season (usually exaggerated, as I would discover) and the ultimate size of the plant (grossly understated, in the case of large growers, to make the commodity seem more suited to the average small garden). At home, with the leafy specimen giving life form to the plant name, I would study the variety in my books. (I had already tried the more direct system of carrying my books to the garden centers — an awkward business, and too conspicuous.)

Not every specimen I brought home was to be found in my books. New Zealand horticulture, with its import-export ties to England, the greatest plant-collecting nation of modern times, and with its Southern Hemisphere proximity to such newer worlds of plants as the outer reaches of its own archipelago, Australia, and South Africa, has grown far too swiftly for the literature ever to keep up. I encountered dozens (and have more recently counted hundreds) of nursery plants not mentioned in the Sunset book, with its basis in the western American gardening experience. New Zealand seems lately to have equaled, or more likely outgrown, our West Coast as one of the world's hotbeds of horticulture.

At the end of the 1970s, several years after I began my New Zealand studies, a new, locally written book appeared, filling in many of the gaps in the Sunset book's plant list. The work is *The New Zealand Illustrated Garden Dictionary,* by Barbara and Lewis Matthews. Yet this book, too, by now omits dozens of still newer plants arriving at garden centers. Even so, both this dictionary and the Sunset book remain invaluable as references. I use them constantly. I also consult the volumes of the Royal Horticultural Society's *Dictionary of Gardening* whenever I can't find a plant, exotic to these islands, in the other books. But often I *still* draw a blank. Horticulture is on the march, the literature tardy.

Gardening With New Zealand Plants, Shrubs and Trees, mentioned earlier on, is a work by Muriel Fisher. First published in 1970, the book has remained steadfastly in print, for reason of having proved to be of constant help to New Zealand gardeners (including me). Until the mid-1980s, Muriel Fisher, together with her husband, William, and son, Malcolm, operated a native plant nursery. (The business ended with the death of William, in his late eighties, and the retirement of Muriel.) On my first visit to Fern Glen, the family nursery, I met Mrs. Fisher, and as offhandedly as I could manage dropped a conversational coin: that I had once written a garden book myself, on the subject of rock gardening, for Sunset Books. This turned out to be the most valuable of credentials and co-incidences, for Malcolm some years previously had bought a copy of my book as a gift for his mother, who was then a beginning rock gardener. She had studied the book, she told me — and now it was to be of service again, as my passport to a friendship with Muriel and her family. (Other New Zealand rock gardeners, including a specialist nurseryman, have told me that they got their start with my book, which sold here for about fifteen years. Allow me this intrusion of pride over some of the most rewarding news I've ever had.)

During the first years of my New Zealand gardening, the late 1970s, I rapidly assembled several hundred kinds of plants, native and non-native. You may remember the item on plants that I included in the garden manifesto I composed for my friends here at the very outset. I would "add foliage plants, and incidentally their flowers, in variety for visual entertainment, and to furnish a study garden of plants suited to the Mediterranean-type climate of Auckland, especially the New Zealand flora."

The garden soon contained far more plants than would have been needed even for full orchestration. What are there, about one hundred musicians in a full symphony orchestra? About the same number of plant players, I would say, make a very full complement for the conductor (the gardener) to handle harmoniously on a smallish property. I had hundreds of players right away in the early years, and in the years since have continued to add species to the garden at a rate of dozens each year. It has required all my skill to maintain any semblance of composition in this garden.

Then there has been the problem of remembering who all the plant players are. Early on, I gave up trying to keep their names fresh in my mind. I started filling a notebook with snippets of each plant I brought into the garden, using cellophane tape to fix each sample and then jotting beside the specimen the plant's name, the year this variety was added to the garden, perhaps the name of the garden center I got it from, certainly the name of the nursery if the plant came from a specialist, and any other facts that would help personify the plant. The notebook is by now quite a sizable if crude herbarium, into which I have had to tip additional pages. I use it as a memory refresher — of rather brief value.

Oh, for a fund of Latin and Greek binomial nomenclature that would pass fluently from the memory to the lips — 'tis a consummation devoutly to be wished. One needs plant names to keep from becoming intellectually lost in one's own garden and, equally important, to keep from seeming a hopeless dotard to one's garden visitors. "What is this one?" the visitor will ask. If he or she is a knowledgeable gardener, and if my memory of the pertinent binomial happens to fail me, then I am forced into lame admission. "Uhhh, can't think of it at the moment. Let me come back to it." (Translation: That's hopeless.) But if my visitor is a novice, he or she almost certainly will not remember the name even if I can recall it, since it is almost impossible to learn binomials by ear; they must be seen on the page, visually engraved on the memory like a cartouche on a temple wall. But for the benefit of the visiting novice, to whom I really owe a plant name, so that he or she may go away satisfied that the meeting has been with a genuine garden guru (hah!), whenever I draw a blank I have no compunction about supplying a pseudonym. "That is a *Recunditum innominatum*," a nameless mystery, I will reply confidently. Asked to name a *second* plant, and again lost, I take only a split second. "That's *Waldenia grandis*" or "*Waldenia pygmaeum*" or "*Waldenia hirsutum*" or "*Waldenia glabrum*," I will pronounce, the species name determined by the plant's being, respectively, big, small, hairy of leaf, or smooth; the generic designation, "Waldenia," is my all-purpose secret weapon, a Latinization of my middle name. But I know next to nothing of Latin syntax, and am uncertain that the *um*'s of the bogus species names are the correct endings to follow the bogus genus. Never mind. My visitor won't really hear, and will go away in good tonic.

I could put labels around, I suppose, but how institutional-appearing, and so many hundreds. A majority would sooner or later disappear, as plant labels will do. All that work of labeling, and still the *Recunditum innominatum*. Perhaps I could work at sharpening my memory by reviewing all the leaves and names in my notebook frequently, say, once every few weeks. But no. The shameful truth is, I'm probably not interested enough in the names to keep them fixed in my mind. My real love is for the textures of plants, and for discovering textural harmonies in plant composition.

An occasion came up recently, though, when I simply had to have hundreds of plant names at the tip of my tongue, or at least at the tip of my fingers. That was the time a young horticulturist from California came by to see the garden. I had met him before in another Aucklander's garden, and had found him to be amazingly well versed in his specialty, New Zealand plants. (He is a staff member at a ten-acre New Zealand garden maintained by the University of California at Santa Cruz.)

I spent two entire mornings — mornings are my regular time for paperwork — preparing for his visit by looking up the names of New Zealand plants in the garden here at Mount Roskill. Poring over my notebook and the gardening books I have mentioned, I wrote down on small sheets of paper the binomials of some 250 kinds of native plants growing in the garden. Then I spent additional hours trekking the garden's thousand-plus feet of pathways, list in hand, linking the names with the living foliages. It was my plan to carry the slips of paper as prompter's cards while guiding my visitor, Tim by name, about the garden. Then, on being asked the name of the plant, as quickly and covertly as possible I would find it by glancing at the list.

And that is somewhat the way things went, except that Tim also asked to be introduced to a few of the several hundred non-natives in the garden. Luckily, the name of the first of these he paused beside, *Leucojum autumnale,* with miniature white bells and grassy blades finer than vermicelli, fairly leaped to mind. (The fact that the name has been disallowed, the plant reclassified by taxonomists more modern than my gardening, didn't faze me; that's the name I learned, and will keep.) I enthused over the bulb's sure return to flower every late summer, to a refined increase in leaf and floriferousness year after year.

My brightness was brief, though, and was followed by a couple of stumbling episodes, the genus recalled easily enough but the species name far out of mind. Then, inevitably, we came to a plant that caused a full mental pratfall — no name whatever. Of course, I would not have dared supply one of my stage names for plants. My probable final grade as a plantsman: C-plus or, I would hope — if my visitor took into account that plants on the whole were growing well — possibly B-minus.

✿

First among the eventual hundreds of plants brought together in this Mount Roskill garden were more than a dozen tall-growing shrubs of various species, all New Zealanders, planted side by side to form hedges. We friends — Mo, the others, and I — were in need of gentrifying screening at two places on the property. Aside from that, I had as always a plantsman's interest in growing and getting to know as many kinds of plants as I could fit together coherently. Coherence — in the mixing of more than twelve kinds of shrubs in two hedges? We shall see.

In home gardening, I've never had much interest in
growing large shrubs spaced out to allow them to develop
in the round, which leads to their obesity and perpetuates
their mood of isolation one from another, even if their
branches eventually touch. Close planting is my preference. This can take the form of an unclipped screen near
the edge of a lot broad enough to accommodate shrubbery
expected to widen to more or less eight feet through, or
the form of clipped hedges, which was the plan for the
screening of this narrow land shelf on which the house
stands. Close planting leads to a comradely aspect in the
garden, and is an effective way of placing a considerable
variety of big growers in a small space. I'm quite content
to have the big boys compete for space, each one develop-
ing a mere few branches in a hedge that is like a linear
bouquet, or a tapestry.

I did not know at the time I planted that in British
gardening there is a term and an appreciation for such mixtures; they are known as tapestry hedges. Those of the
British, not quite as mixed as mine, consist of two or three
kinds of plants hedged together. It is a controversial sort
of gardening to some, to whom the name is a mere eu-
phemism for wildish carryings-on in the hedgerows.

The unbelievers have a point. Most tapestry hedges in
Britain appear to me to have begun as upstarting wildness
in the garden — as a result of birds dropping the seed of
hawthorn, for example, while perched in a hedge of yew
or some other plant. The seed germinates, the two plants
commingle, and if left together become inseparable Sia-

mese, not to be reft apart without leaving ugly gaps in the facade of the hedge. But lo and behold, the two, or in some cases three, distinct foliages mixed in the hedge make — to some eyes at least — a curiously beautiful marriage or ménage, which we might as well enjoy for what it is.

The surprise demonstrated here, that of plants inventing their own compositions, is one of the great forces in garden art. Plants will meet unpredictably in any garden that is not too closely guarded, and will often set up unplanned harmonies. The gardener need only be liberal enough to recognize a good thing coming and then let it happen. Accidental meetings of plants may sometimes result in intolerable entanglements, but just as often they turn out to be the life of the garden, the happiest and most exciting events taking place there.

Ergo the origin of the tapestry hedge. In purposely planting one, I find that smallish leaves, up to two or three inches long, are usually the easiest to combine attractively. Differences in leaf forms within the hedge are not discordant, since their small size provides a readily unifying feature. Yet sometimes the wildest combinations of foliages — disparate sizes as well as shapes and colors — can be the most dramatically beautiful. Birds or other natural agents are the usual instigators. A certain tapestry hedge I've seen involves an arborvitae (*Thuja plicata*) and a maple (*Acer rubrum*). Theirs was undoubtedly an accidental meeting, the maple having twirled in as a samara on the breeze and having come to rest and germination at the base of a line of young arborvitae. The differing trees have grown up together, to about fifteen feet tall, as a parti-colored green wall, darker and lighter, mapley and conifer-fine of foliage. In autumn the particoloring intensifies, with the reddening of the maple leaves. This leafy facade separates a home garden from a street corner. The gardener who lives behind this living wall clips it loosely, only enough to keep the trees out of traffic. He seems appreciative of being custodian of a masterwork of spontaneous garden art.

I myself have not dared attempt any such unaccountable hedge harmonies here at Mount Roskill. I have opted for safer associations of such smallish foliages as lemon-wood (*Pittosporum eugenioides*), mirror plant (*Coprosma repens*), tahinu (*Pomaderris phylicifolia*), parapara (*Pseudopanax lessonii*), and other trees or shrubs of the New Zealand botany. The Maori plant names tahinu and parapara, by the way, are pronounced with Polynesian vowel sounds: ah eh ee oh ooh. I use these common names since the plants have none in English. Not being a gardener for whom plant names in any language come trippingly off the tongue, I'm a bit awed that most New Zealanders of European descent know a great many of the native plants by their Maori names (without knowing the Maori language). These are the names in everyday use, even by those gardeners who know the equivalent Latin.

My plantings of tahinu, parapara, and all, set out as four-and-a-half-footers at an average three and a half feet apart, have grown satisfyingly into privacy hedges. But it

has taken time. The lower, hence the more rapidly rewarding, of the two hedges required three years to reach the
needed height of nine feet. That was the hedge I planted
close to the front of the house, in the only available strip
of unconcreted ground.

The Fence Lady, a friendly neighbor of whom I've spoken — the one who said go ahead and tear it down —
seemed to be puzzled by this other project of mine.
I would guess that in her neighboring years she had got
used to looking directly from her living-room window into
the corresponding window of our house. Now she ex-
pressed tactful concern about the rising hedge and the
sinking abode. "My, that certainly is *growing*," she said of
my hedge, at about the end of year two, her clear tone and
meaning being "When are you going to cut it?" Yes, I
agree with my neighbor that it is usually best not to pur-
dah the front of a house with solid leafage. However, there
were special circumstances. The deck is the only livable
area outdoors at the front of the property. Here a hedge
sufficiently tall now makes a cozy screen between us and
the bustling world.

Livable outdoor space is to me the ultimate luxury in
home life, and if you were to call on me early in the morning, you might well find me seated behind the hedge in
our deck garden, with my mug of morning tea in hand.
I'm usually seated here again in the evening, undergoing a
kind of psychic transition from outdoors to indoors person.
Here I will be for half an hour in the long summer evening, a time of day when I'm pleasantly used up from an

141

afternoon's work or puttering in the garden but unready to give up on the day and the outdoors. The deck garden is my halfway house, part carpentry, part foliage and open air. I daresay the quality of a day in the lives of any of us who spend even a few minutes in this garden is enhanced. A great amount of living takes place here on a tiny raft: The deck that is the garden's platform measures only twenty-three by seven feet. On it grow plants in plenty to provide reading material for the reader of leaves, buds, and flowers — about seventy-one varieties grouped in containers (I arrive at a different total every time I try to count up). In addition, there are the several different plants in the tapestry hedge, the hedge that was three years growing to provide the green embrace of this garden room.

It took eight years for the hedge I planted at the uphill side of the house to do its job, at fourteen feet in height. As a matter of diplomatic good fortune, the neighboring houses uphill stood far enough away (about 150 to 200 feet) and high enough above that I was able to screen them out without blocking their view over the top of our house and the tree canopy of the ravine to the parklike golf course. The closest uphill neighbor, a newcomer, seemed almost as interested in planting for privacy as I. He suggested that I plant my hedge on the uphill side of the five-foot-high concrete-block retaining wall that separated the two properties. That way we could shorten our wait for privacy by a couple of years. I declined, partly out of concern that the wall could be ruptured by the pressure of woody roots thickening with several years' growth. He went ahead and put in his own hedge of rooted cuttings of pencil willows (*Salix chilensis*). His hedge grew, as willows will, powerfully; all that willow power, in this fastigiate tree, directed upward like a rocket, gave twelve feet of height — more than enough — in about three years. But within eight years the trees had grown too bare of trunk to be a screen, and had become muscular enough of root to be dangerous to the wall. The trees stood eighteen inches from the concrete-block bulwark; for safety, the distance should have been at least several yards. I asked our neighbor if he would cut the trees, and he obliged. There was no loss of privacy to either of us, for in eight years my tapestry hedge had fulfilled its task. (To keep the hedge at an ideal height of fourteen feet, I prune it annually with hand tools while standing on an aluminum ladder as tall as the hedge.)

The same uphill neighbor planted a second hedge along a side of his property paralleling a long downhill drive that serves several houses, including ours. His planting was of a vanload of bamboo divisions (*Bambusa glaucescens*) that a friend had given him for the grubbing out. His hedge grew up a beauty, to about sixteen feet in height in only three years or so. He planted the bamboo rather too far apart, however, at three-foot intervals. Several years passed before the line of canes increased to form a solid barrier, one that would keep in the German shepherd the family brought home as a pup. Even so, the planter of bamboo seemed to me pretty smart with his tall hedge — only three years to glory.

I had doubts about the good sense of my own eight-year wait for a serviceable hedge built of slower plants. But now that that wait is well in the past, and now that I've had adequate years of experience with both his planting and mine, I feel not so scooped after all. At sixteen limber feet, the bamboo hedge — which the planter preferred to leave at full height — arched out over the driveway it aligned, and on rainy days would bow down, impeding cars. Vehicles could barely scrape past. Besides the problem of the mature, flopping canes, the new canes, asparagusing up in the strip of grass lawn that separates the bamboo from the concrete driveway, are a nuisance on mowing days. Books I've read say that mowing off bamboo sprouts to control the spreading of the plant is an easy business. Hardly. A bumpiness of ground goes with the arising sprouts and stops the mower dead, as do the stiff culm shields of the bamboo, shucked off as the plant sends up new poles. The bamboo hedge is four ways a mess, taking into consideration also the constantly dropped leaves.

After twelve years in residence, the bamboo planter and his family moved away. The new people who moved in quickly noted all the problems that came with the hedge and decided that although they needed the screening, they could curtail the worst habit of the bamboo, the lolling into the drive in rainy weather, by having it pruned. The problem has indeed been completely cured by the foreshortening of the bamboo stems; the other bad habits — the bumpy roots, the dropped stem shields and leaves — remain as before. I would love this hedge if there weren't lawn at the base of the bamboo, lawn at the driveway side, which I try to maintain.

Bamboo as hedging (or as a grove) is best planted far away from grass that is to be kept neat. Near the bases of my own bamboo plantings, a path or shrubbery provides a place on or into which the bamboo can harmlessly rain down its leaves and other droppings. Here at Mount Roskill, I've planted a screen of the tall-growing *Bambusa oldhamii* along a path in the ravine immediately below the house. When I first came to this property, the narrow land shelf that supports the house dropped off ominously, only five feet from a corner of the building. The bamboo planted along the garden path below has helped stabilize the none-too-reliable hillside. Its deep and closely interlocking root system holds the soil in the manner of steel mesh over steep rocks.

From its subterranean base the bamboo sends up a sturdy palisade of canes as thick as a strongman's arm. Over the bank — and against these canes — we have tossed pruned branches and weed harvests these many years. The bamboo holds all this jetsam securely, and as straight up and down as if it were in a bin. By now the piled material — most of it in decayed and compacted condition — has built the hillside outward from the original five feet to eleven feet from the house, deterring soil erosion. The material has another value: as a glorious compost heap, six feet in width, twenty-one feet in length, ten feet in height. The pile is one of two on the property, of approximately equal size. The total quantity is far greater than we could ever spread or dig into the garden soil. Nevertheless, it is good to have and to think on. Inwardly, I smile like a Marcos at such an embanked fortune, delighting in its stupendous excess.

From time to time, I mine for garden use a mere yard or so of the inexhaustible compost, digging down beneath the newer green and browning layers to obtain wheelbarrow-loads of fluffy blackish goods, still warm with the bacterial processes of its conversion from vegetation to a more mineralized condition. Like almost any other gardener who collects and heaps garden detritus, I have become an inspired rotter, rather in love with this stuff called compost — or, called by its wilderness names, leaf mold, duff, humus — a substance betokening earthly health in its color, texture, and aroma.

In my attraction to this planetary manna, I have gained a sense of camaraderie with the garden's hedgehogs. Hedgehogs burrow into my compost heaps at dawn for a day-long nap, and in autumn for a winter's sleep. The animal, a beloved hedgerow inhabitant in Britain, was brought to New Zealand by early British settlers for sentimental remembrance. Every time I see a hedgehog, it almost seems to me to be wearing a little Union Jack. Except once.

Once in May (late autumn), while mining away at the compost with a garden fork, I extracted from the pile — what on earth? — a ball of green moss, it appeared to be, until the ball unfurled into a stubby loaf of legs, trunk, and head, scurried off a few yards, and reentered the compost heap at a point safely distant from me. It was a hedge-hog, which, before turning in for the winter, had evidently barrel-rolled in a variety of feathery moss that grows (wel-comely) in the garden's shadier areas of lawn, filling in for the failing grass. Rolling in the moss, the hedgehog had gathered a downy winter quilt on its spines. Sleep green, sleep tight, my little bryophyte.

I went back to my compost mining. What bounty! The garden's two treasuries of mostly mellowed, ready-for-use compost total about 180 cubic yards: call it an even 200. As branches newly cut and weeds newly pulled, the vegetal mass was vastly greater, perhaps five times as much. In the decade and a half I've been at work here, the biomass removed from this not very large, partly wooded garden (to keep order and maintain open, sunny spaces) must by now amount to 1000 cubic yards. The plant ma-terial, a springy, airy mass at the time of removal and pil-ing, was weighty even so, at least 100 pounds per yard. That's fifty tons, in the thousand yards of excess vegetation gathered up and carried out of the garden. We gardeners really are splendid creatures.

Those of us who may be inclined to install idealized marmoreal specimens in the garden should forget all the statuary likes of Persephone, Pan, and others of the Gre-cian panegyry and put up one with a prouder title, "The Gardener," chiseled on the plinth. Not too much of the forked animal, if you please. The more fig leaves the bet-ter, to the degree of a figure as generalized as Rodin's Bal-zac enwrapped in his cloak — the gardener as crag and

cloud, as Olympian as can be. Or the gardener as compost mound, why not? — a divine heap, all receiving, all
benefitting.

Back at one of the garden's heaps, I shall now throw on
some spicy-scented cypress branches cut from the tallest of
our hedges. The number-one contributor to the biomass in
the compost piles has been our hedge of *Cupressus macrocarpa,* planted by the former owner of the house about
twenty-five years ago. This tree species is the celebrated
macrocarpa of British gardening and literature, with a
place in the works of writers as diverse as Margery Fish and
Noël Coward. It is an old-fashioned kind of hedge in today's New Zealand, a suburban descendant from agricul-
tural New Zealand. In the nineteenth century and the first
half of the twentieth, macrocarpa, a California native, and
two other West Coast American conifers, *Thuja plicata*
and *Pinus radiata,* all numbered among the foremost
hedgerow-windbreak plantings in the country. These days
few New Zealanders plant macrocarpa. Suburban gardeners
especially seem warned away by the colossal crown spread
and the roots flexing out of the ground in maturing specimens of the tree in the countryside.

As an antiquarian, I'm pleased to have had the experience of working with this plant, historic in horticulture.
Believe me, I have worked. When I first arrived, I found a
line of macrocarpa trees unpruned for years, feral conifers
with swooping branches that had ingested power lines and
that grated against the house in a wind. At twenty-six feet
in height, the hedge was way out of control, perhaps to

the point of no return. Should I cut it down or cut it back to size, chancing its death or at best its slow regeneration to a full green front? I decided I had nothing to lose in attempting the restoration of the hedge and in trying to avoid the complete removal of the trees, tons of wood.

I don't recommend my method, but it worked this once. I sawed off branches as thick as six inches, to impose a squared-off formality and reasonable dimensions on the hedge, leaving it shockingly stubbed and denuded. Would the macrocarpa come back, nice and full? It has, slowly, over a period of years, except for a couple of scars still healing. Now maintained as a two-story, dark green wall, the hedge forms an effective backdrop for my complex broadleaf planting in the foreground — groves of titoki trees (*Alectryon excelsus*), assorted shrubs, and perennials with bold foliage; boldest of all is a plant with yard-long, pleated, straplike leaves, *Wachendorfia thyrsiflora*.

Macrocarpa, held in this hedge at a height and width of eighteen by eight feet, has sufficient interior space for the dead inside foliage to drop clear away to the ground. This natural clearance obviates the macrocarpa tragedy discussed by Margery Fish in *We Made a Garden,* the tendency of hedges made of this tree to die at the young age of about fifteen, choked to death by old brown leaves stuffed up within the congested, tightly pruned branches.

The maintenance of our macrocarpa hedge is a yearly major event in my garden life, a job done entirely with hand tools, which leave the softer outline I prefer. I begin to think about it months in advance, while I'm doing a little gentle work with pruning shears in my container plant garden in Manila. I wonder if I can possibly still be in good enough shape, or get myself in condition, to climb that ladder one more season and perform all those *tai chi* pruning acrobatics, slow stretchings out to the full while poised on a rung of aluminum. But I do complete the task. It is my yearly declaration of youth.

Job done, I have been asked how by my Auckland friends Bruce and Albert, both of whom maintain hedges (of lilly-pilly and lemonwood) less than half the height of the macrocarpa by using rented power hedge-cutters. Let me gloat over this: Both these men have asked me, on separate occasions when they have come to visit, *in exactly the same words* and impressed tone, "How did you do that?" With patience, perseverance, and a dash of derring-do (my motto as a gardener).

8

Conquering
Concrete

ALL ALONG, I've conducted a pitched battle in this garden with my worthy aesthetic opponent "Mr. Gray," as I call him, the chap who installed prodigious amounts of concrete on the Mount Roskill lot at the time he built the house a quarter-century ago. I understand that he was a contractor in concrete work and is now long gone from this city. Yet he is always here in his generous calling card, which brings him to mind. I imagine him as the personification of his professional medium, a solid citizen and tidy personage with carefully combed graying hair, dressed for his job in well-ironed coveralls (gray, of course), on his way in a pickup truck (same color), with a slogan on the door:

Gray *Un*limited
Artist in Concrete

He has given me, a Mr. Green, much to do. The property as he left it was a concrete fortress, with such overwhelming stacks and spreads of the stuff as five concrete block walls and a front yard almost totally concreted.

People must have a place to park their cars, of course, but not, if I could help it, the *whole* place. There at the front Mr. Gray had spread fifty by fifty feet of his specialty. Along two sides of the concrete, a few feet of ground had been given over to strips of grass and weeds in hard soil, usable as auxiliary parking space. At its far end, the concrete pad stretched to within nine inches of the property line — exactly where leafy screening from the neighborhood seemed to me sorely needed, yet impossible. The nine-inch-wide strip of available soil supported a fence of concrete posts and chain-link steel (the one I've written of having condemned and sledgehammered and hacksawed down). The parking pad approached at its near end to within sixteen inches of the deck at the front of the house. The intervening strip of ground held a row of wretched tea roses that had limped for some years down a slow road of neglect. They held out few leaves and no flowers on blackened limbs that seemed to beg for a merciful end to it all. I, with my grub hoe, soon granted that mercy. (In their place would go the deck garden's crucial hedge.)

Leading from the parking pad, an eight-foot-wide concrete walk (that's right, eight feet wide — I could hardly believe it) extended along a narrow side yard and across the back of the house, where it snugly fitted up against plastic foundation paneling sprayed with gray Gunite to simulate concrete. Mr. Gray was a true aficionado. If he couldn't use the real stuff, he provided a facsimile.

His five concrete block walls were magnificent works of craftsmanship, the largest of them eight feet high by

fifty feet long. I'll give him this: In his work with concrete
blocks, he was a master of joinery, as neat as an Incan
stonemason. In my years of gardening here, I would, with
a green will equal to the determination of His Grayness,
cover nearly all his stolidly magnificent wallworks with
vegetation: with small-leaved ivies and another clinging
vine, *Metrosideros carmineus,* whose leaves are rounded and
as small as peas, held flat and tight against the wall surface;
with a billowy perennial, *Plectranthus australis,* which has
spilled over the highest wall, top to bottom, in full shade;
with many shrubs planted along the sunnier walls and
loosely pruned to keep them casually close to the walls'
faces (*Pseudopanax lessonii* is one of my favorites in this use).

Several linear yards of Mr. Gray's highest wall — a
curved portion which, considering the square blockiness of
the material, is masterfully graded and smooth — I have
left mostly bare, in admiration of his workmanship. Here
the airborne spores of certain mosses native to stony cliffs
have found a compatible surface on which to take hold
and grow. As greenery, they have become as valuable a
textural note in the garden as any of its plants higher on
the scale of life. Other plants associated with the wall are
the vine *Metrosideros carmineus*; a down-draping *Monstera
deliciosa,* with snaky arms dressed in familiar leaves (this
plant is the "split-leaf philodendron" of indoor gardening);
and three plants in containers atop the wall. These include the bromeliad *Aechmea* 'Royal Wine', with purplish
strap leaves, one of the most self-sufficient plants I've ever
known. It requires no watering or fertilizing in open-air

gardening (it is also an easy house plant) and increases its
rosettes steadily in its container for years, or until I break
the plant apart, as I have done three times in a decade, to
gain starts for other plantings. The other containers hold
the epiphytic fern *Asplenium flaccidum,* native to the ravine
on this land, depending from tree trunks as from this wall
top, with down-growing fronds as much as three feet long;
and another New Zealand perching plant found high up in
the branch crooks of mature trees, *Collospermum hastatum,* a
heavy nest of strap-form leaves, which windstorms occasionally dislodge. We found this collospermum crashed on
the ground sometime in the 1970s. Brought home, the
plant has grown happily ever since, balanced on the wall
top, braced with a few big rocks; for food, it has leaf mold
rammed in between the stones at the time of planting.
This is a male plant, the showier in flower of the two
sexes, with an inflorescence like a bunch of foot-long, fuzzy
blond caterpillars. Nearby on the same wall perches a female of the species, bearer of orange-yellow berries in pen-
dant cobs.

My green answer to the property's horizontal stretches
of concrete has been the same as for the walls: Cover them.
I grow plants on the overly broad walks and the parking
pad wherever possible, reserving minimal areas for traffic.
Mr. Gray had it the other way around: minimal planting
area, maximal paving.

In addition to the eight-foot-wide concrete boulevard
at the side and back of the house, there were other walk-
ways, a two-footer that extended like a scar across the patch

of grass in the back yard and a four-footer incongruously laid down in a wooded part of the property. I covered both these sidewalks with about three inches of loamy soil; the sidewalk in the woods also received a scattering of sawdust on top of the loam. The grass lawn immediately began inching out over the concrete of the narrower walk, muffling it completely and erasing it from view in two years' time. Nowadays, when I run a lawn mower over "X marks the spot," as crime reporters used to say, where the sidewalk was, I smile like a contented killer at my buried secret. And the sidewalk in the woods is now a sawdust path, woodland brown, with stoloniferous ferns and selaginella creeping out over its edges.

In the early years of the garden, I placed plain wooden planters purchased at a garden center toward the edges of the eight-foot sidewalk. As landscaping, and as concrete-taming, the job was fairly successful, if a bit stiff — crude wood on crude concrete — until the ivies and other weeping plants planted along with upright growers went into their romantic swoon down over the sides of the tubs. We maintained these plantings for years, but eventually found it impossible to supply enough water to keep the plants thrifty during summer drought.

To see what was going on at the roots, I eased several of the containers over on their sides and tugged the plantings out of the boxes. The plants came out with a solid block of clenched roots and soil, and a couple of shocks for me. The bottom two-fifths of each extracted mass was powdery dry. Roots so congested the soil that they prevented water from finding its way to the bottom. At the very bottom of the soil mass, ants, the bane of container gardening in this country and in others, tiny ants by the thousands, had excavated extensive galleries and were now racing about in a disaster panic. I could live with the ants — have been doing so everywhere in the world I garden — except for one of their practices, that of bringing in ant cows (root aphids), which suck the sap of one's container plants while the ants lap up the honeydew of the aphids. It's a marvelous symbiosis perfected by nature, which unfortunately is murderous to container plants. They are caught in their container like a dog on a leash, with nowhere to escape into uncontaminated ground. The ants and the aphids love dry soil conditions at the bottom of containers; much less to their liking is soil kept constantly moist.

All right. I had an idea. I would try placing earth for plants directly on the concrete in nestlike containers of natural stones pieced together — four sides of stone, but only the concrete at the bottom. The concrete would draw moisture steadily downward into itself, and help prevent the formation of a bottom zone of soil dryness attractive to ants and ant cows. On the broad walk, I used large stones to form the containers, setting them up in dry-wall construction, of course, since I am anti-concrete. I shaped a number of these rock pots, all at least a foot high, varying from a squarish four feet in diameter to an oblong eight feet.

For a soil mix: loam, decayed sawdust, hoof-and-horn

fertilizer. For plants: the toughest of big foliages — plants I had found to be especially tolerant of life in containers and sufficiently architectonic of leaf to stand up tellingly in the sterile setting of concrete. Within rock pots located in morning sun I arranged *Phormium tenax* 'Burgundy', bronzy and sword-bladed of leaf, to six feet tall; *Astelia banksii,* a huge, silvery, grasslike clump; tall-growing cymbidiums; and that common, tough, and worthy fern of world gardening in warm countries, my vulgar old matey, *Nephrolepis cordifolia.* But even these leafy brutes were not quite enough to balance the built-in concrete-and-clapboard back-yardiness of the setting. So I've used some plain tan wall hangings woven of pandanus by Mo to back up the plantings with rich texture, intermediate and linking in their alliances to the architecture of the wall and the sculptural shapes of the mural plants. In a shadier location, the rock-pot planting features bromeliads of the genus *Neoregelia,* with their pineapple-top leaf rosettes in shades of plum red, tan, pale green, and brick pink.

These experimental plantings on concrete have done themselves proud, to use an American country expression. Everything has been growing well for years — no going back, only ahead. As long as we pour on the water, especially on those plants growing in the desert under the eaves, and add fertilizer several times a year, I think we can expect a burgeoning future for these pot gardens. However, I have found that almost no pot plant can be grown forever without the eventual necessity — in five years, ten, or twenty — of either dividing the specimen or pruning its roots and then replanting it in fresh soil. When the plant begins to appear stunted, the time has come for refurbishment.

As to the artistry of this experiment, sometimes when I look, I like what I see. At other times, I don't. At any rate, this opus is the closest thing to a silk purse that I could make out of a sow's ear of an architectural setting.

I used rocks to make containers because at the time I had rocks to work with. During an earlier gardening period, I used railroad ties to shape plant beds directly on top of the concrete parking pad at the front of the house. The ties came from Australia. In the 1970s, that country tore up many country miles of early twentieth-century railroad track and ties, the latter made of ironbark eucalyptus. The island continent found a market among New Zealand gardeners for boatloads of the ties, of a durable wood attractively silvered with age.

On top of Gray Square, in the front garden these years, planting beds framed with railroad ties support the choicest of small plants we grow, which we cannot keep alive anywhere else. The beds are snail-proof — oases in a concrete desert unattainable to the mollusks. They lack the slime-power to make their needed trailway over this much concrete, to reach the framed beds and ravage the (to them) exquisitely delicious rock fern, *Cheilanthes humilis*. This species grows as a four-inch-tall grove of leathery, firm grayish green fronds, each like a minute but mature spruce tree. The plant came to me as a gift from Muriel Fisher, the gardening author and pteridologist, who collected it at

its only station within Auckland, a lava cliff near the summit of Mount Roskill, of all places, only a mile from the
garden. The fern is abundant there. The framed bed in our
garden provides this lowland "alpine," and other, true
mountaineers, their demanded full sun and rapid drainage,
in an especially gritty soil mix within a raised bed.

Safe within a tie bed is another refugee from the demon
with stalked eyes: the miniature bulb flower *Oxalis purpurea*
'Alba'. Here in the autumn sun, the plant opens satiny
white goblets of an unbelievable bigness, which reminds
me of the stemless gentian; like that flower, the oxalis gob-
let is at first perfectly sessile and upright, later ascending
on a bit of stem. The flowers are presented as a posy within
a circle of grayish cloverlike leaves pressed flat on the bed's
surface of pure crushed stone.

Why, I wonder, is this plant not one of the more famous rock garden miniatures? It is one of the very loveli-
est, and easiest to grow, and surest to flower year after year,
of the more than one thousand species of rock garden
plants I have grown in a near half-century of gardening. In
fact, the plant remains a rarity. Mo found it once, years
ago, in an Auckland garden center; I've never seen it for
sale anywhere. It may remain an exile from gardens because
of the onus of its name, *Oxalis,* a scary genus suggesting
only terrible weeds to most gardeners. In the case of *Oxalis
purpurea,* this is a tricky consideration. The ordinary form,
a rose-colored beauty, is a moderate spreader, capable of
invading lawn grass. But its albino form, 'Alba', stays in a
close clump and never wanders.

In the early 1980s, in a proselytizing phase of my New Zealand gardening, I gave bulbs of *Oxalis purpurea* 'Alba' to several nurseries in western America. I went about it with the spread-the-good-news compulsion of a Johnny Appleseed handing out pages of Scripture with his gifts of pips. By now the oxalis may be more readily available — to my proud regret. There is a poignancy in giving rare plants. Their rarity is like virginity, a thing diminished to the extent of its disbursal. Ah well, it leads to friendships.

The oxalis and the rock fern are but two of the many sanctuary plants in the oases beds on concrete. In horticultural terms, the framed beds are a success; they are equally so as a landscape asset. They break up the barrenness of a stretch of concrete I found insufferable. But oh, how some of my friends, the beloved philistines in my life, arriving by car, have grumbled over these island beds, despite the fact that they are reasonably situated at one end of the parking area, nearly out of the way, requiring of drivers only a little extra jockeying. But listen to the scolding. You would think that cars and maximum convenience in parking are sacred and a preference for plants quite odd. (By the way, I had the blessing of the property owner in building these beds. Mo had purchased and potted up a collection of miniature bulb flowers, including the oxalis. The beds were built partly to make a safe haven for the bulbs.)

Another of my counterattacks on the concrete is a bed of titoki trees (*Alectryon excelsus*) and other plants built out several feet over the edge of the former parking area. Plants lushly serene now occupy the space, almost erasing from my mind the major embarrassment I experienced in building this bed.

I had had two eight-yard truckloads of topsoil dumped here to make a raised garden. After shoveling and shaping the soil as far out over the concrete as I dared, taking into account the absolute demands of traffic, I retained the two-foot-high, embanked edge of the soil with stones, then planted the trees and all. Soon afterward I went away for the winter — my annual departure.

I had gone and left a great mistake in gardening. The soil had absorbed several autumn rains at the time it was delivered. Over winter, with continuing rains, the built-up soil became oozy. Mo wrote to me that my stone-and-soil construct wobbled like a jelly when booted — as was necessary. The big, heavy stones of the rock face (now a rock dam) in front of the earthwork required a cautious kicking back into line after every rainstorm. The wall did hold through the winter, but it was touch and go. I still suffer grim twinges in thinking how close was the spilling out of the new garden over the entire parking pad — a ghastly gravy of mud, trees, stones, and disgrace.

The problem cured itself during the next spring and summer. The sickly mud reconstituted into healthily textured earth. While increasingly dry weather allowed the mud slowly to give up its soak of water, New Zealand's Brobdingnagian earthworms (as long as sixteen inches in the Auckland area, three feet in other parts of the country) burrowed through and through the soil, reestablishing a porosity thumped out of it in the bulldozing, trucking, and dumping process. The trees, too, helped in making the soil cohesive, as any plant will, by clutching soil particles with growing roots and siphoning up free moisture.

The embanked garden has never again turned to mud. The low rock wall has become not only firm but stubbornly set, as unmortared stonework will do within a year or two of being constructed. I always worry over stones that insist on being slightly wobbly at first, no matter how exactingly set into place and tightened with hammered-in wedges in the form of small stones. But time, worms, and roots work their work. Recently, it took all my strength in pulling on a pry bar of steel to dislodge several of the stones in the wall, in order to plant clumps of a native ornamental grass (*Chionochloa flavicans*) on the wall face — a late thought.

There is a moral to this story: For heaven's sake, don't attempt to build a raised stone-retained garden with wet soil, especially not at the beginning of winter rains. Wait for the drier weather of late spring or summer.

9

The Neighbors

THE NEIGHBORS, damn them. They are the trolls in one's garden life, waiting in ambush just beyond one's border. The neighbors, bless them, for the paragons of considerateness and cooperation they are. They've left a little plastic bag of homegrown lemon cucumbers at the foot of our door, a gesture of comradeship, of clanship even, as caring as that of a cat, who would leave in this same spot, sure to be noticed, a tidbit of its own harvesting — the crunched-off head and forelegs of a lizard, for instance (an actual gift from a cat to me). I'm not sure I will dine on either of these offerings, but I'm touched.

On the whole in my suburban life here and there about the world, I've been amazingly lucky with neighbors. In several places I've made garden friends across the boundary, leading to the coordination of our landscaping; or we have agreed to eradicate, physically and psychologically, the line separating the two properties and have combined them into a somewhat communal garden. Here on Mount Roskill, our neighbor Mike and I have such a garden under way.

During the first years after Mike moved in (succeeding the kindly Fence Lady), he and I — both of us busy gardeners — always said hello cordially but watched each other warily, I'm sure, each hoping the other would not send over invasions of shade, roots, or falling leaves on the upper, sunnier parts of the properties. Down below, we were independently at work on the same job, trailblazing and planting in the ravine. I had begun years ahead of Mike, who was in fact at work on his first garden. Eager for usable landscape examples, he approached me one day and asked if he and his friend Marge could walk through the garden. Of course they could: The garden is there to be shared. And so our friendship began.

Mike was a newcomer from England. Marge, Maori in ancestry, was of the oldest of all New Zealand stock. They had met in a local Mormon church. (Many of the Maori belong; the faith has long been an active seeker of souls in New Zealand, as it has throughout the Pacific.) I walked my paths with them, acting the host, introducing them to plants. I suggested that we connect the pathways Mike had been constructing on his place with those I'd already laid out in my area. We would gain a double-size garden for walking and viewing. They liked the idea. I, having more spare time than they, at once blazed and shoveled the pathway splices connecting both properties.

Now occasionally I hear Mike and Marge, alone or with company, on the paths below me; I hear them talking about this or that plant, and am gratified to have a garden that people find worth visiting. I hear them but don't see them down there, where native trees screen them from view, adding a perfecting dignity to our strollers' agreement.

On the lower hillside we now share, my garden paths are mostly darkish, with trees locking overhead and with ferns and broad-leaved subtropical forest plants at foot and shoulder. My shadowy trails lead directly to Mike's sunnier pathways and into color explosions at pathside, of such extravagant flowers as the hybrids of *Fuchsia triphylla* and the entire color range of *Impatiens holstii,* the three-foot shrublike form of busy Lizzie. Busy indeed: a basket of flowers, pink, white, rose, salmon, or candy-striped, every day, spring until winter. I delight in the excess, for it is not of my making. I can enjoy it as if I were six or eight years old again, with none of the troubling hauteur of gardening sophistication. I would seem to have grown ever more narrowly the naif, stultified by convention, while Mike works as a patternist and colorist more in line with such modern garden fauvists as Roberto Burle Marx, planter of swirling, polychromatic "color spots." Such influences, once admitted to the life of an old digger like myself, shaped by the propriety of harmonious colors and the perceived evil of clash, are life-extending. Through their work I have lengthened my own garden life by perceptible decades or even centuries. Quite often I obtain the feeling of having lived several lifetimes through my enjoyment of the work of other gardeners, as different as taste and available plants can make them.

One wavers, though, in such resolve to keep an open

mind. I didn't grieve at all when a New Guinea impatiens Mike planted along a path exactly at our boundary — a plant with magenta flowers over variegated yellow-and-green leaves — died from chill in its second winter. And yet, I have since found the same color selection of New Guinea impatiens at garden centers in several countries, and have thought this tribally wild plant daub of a plant quite handsome. Perhaps I could place it.

Mike and Marge and I were to share another, more ambitious garden project: a rock garden or, more exactly, a rockery. There is a difference, as I said in the book I wrote on rock gardening many years ago. I've just looked up my earlier self, and will paraphrase that fellow: The rock garden is a carefully staged art form, a supposedly natural landscape of rocks and harmonious small wildflowers that might be found in a stony wilderness, whereas the rockery is usually a garden area where stonework is used more for retaining than for ornament, and is planted with anything the gardener would have there.

Lawn covered the hillside where Mike proposed a garden of plants and rocks; he did say "rock garden," and even though I can't concur with the use of the term, in light of what happened, I'll use it for now. He asked my advice on the practicality of putting in a rock garden in place of a thirty-by-fifty-foot, sunny expanse of grass, on a hillside so steep that mowing was nearly impossible. He would slip and fall to his knees or sitzmark nearly every time, and lose his grip on the power mower. Real danger there.

I replied that weeding and grooming a rock garden

would take more time than mowing the area. But yes, certainly, a rock garden would be more practical than continuing his risk of injury in mowing. So we nodded in agreement over installing such a garden. I volunteered to help out, Mike having allowed that he had no idea how to go about the work.

Over a period of weeks following, my neighbor brought home and piled quite a tonnage of volcanic rock, from an Auckland quarry that lets people come on weekends to load up vans or trailers or, in Mike's case, an old sedan dented and rusty beyond concern about additional damage by the brutal stones. The bigger the better, I had told him. And he, a powerfully built young man, brought home some really meaningful stones, up to three feet across (but flattish) — attractively aged-appearing specimens, to boot. (Auckland's quarry rocks, a ferruginous, roughly surfaced scoria, do not look freshly quarried.)

With stones enough in stockpiles, we were ready for the campaign. I decided not to bother desodding the area. Instead, we covered the lawn with newspapers about ten sheets thick, to smother the grass. On top of the papers we spread about a ten-inch depth of used mushroom compost, black and crumbly. Mike obtained it very cheaply, low cost being a necessary factor, and we were to find that the material had a steroid effect on everything we planted. The plants all turned into giants of their species, overpowering some kinds of weeds. The power in the plants has not run down even now, five years later, with no additional fertilizing.

Placing garden rock, either in the duty position of soil retaining or in the ornamental work of rock gardening, is slow, precise work. Our job called for both kinds of rock arrangement, as retaining walls in some places, in others as groupings of stones simulating natural outcrop. In both situations, key stones had to be nestled well down in the mulch and all stones locked together for stability. The work took up several hours each of several days. I was the lead horse, with Mike and Marge helping to tussle the weightiest stones into place.

As designer, I tried to keep from appearing dogmatic, and turned over to Mike and Marge entirely the design and construction of a retaining embankment of stone. I have a pleasant memory of this: the absorption, even excitement, evident in their voices as they worked, placing the heavy jigsaw pieces that irregular stones become in the puzzle of fitting stone to stone.

At last we three had made good design sense of every stone in Mike's stockpiles. We raked smooth the garden's soil surfaces between the stoneworks, stood back for a gaze, and pronounced the job a great success. The day was hot, and, still gazing, we shared a self-congratulatory round of iced lemonade.

With rocks nobly placed, the site was ready to be turned into either a rock garden or a rockery, depending on the planting. I might as well cut my writing short, for you can readily divine Mike's planting scheme: anything and everything. It is good for what it is. I'm finding a lot of fun lately in being a visual participant in his hyper-colorful rockery.

Several of the flowers Mike planted are among my own favorites, for their incredible willingness and generosity as well as their beauty. One such is *Erigeron karvinskianus,* native to Mexican mountains. Now it is one of the tell-tale plants of British horticulture: Wherever in the world the British empire expanded, this plant traveled along as part of the garden culture, and soon escaped the garden, air-borne by its parachute seeds. Throughout the ruin of the raj, the plant carries on, a naturalized citizen, to be found among other roadside wildings, especially on rocks. It re-members Mexico, and seeks rocky aeries on cliffs or out-crops, where it takes hold so toughly as to withstand the most xerophytic conditions for months. It has made itself the royal Brittanic weed, one that I pull out of the rockery where it threatens other plants and allow to grow where it is of help.

The nearly year-round generosity of this plant's flower-ing is especially welcome in late autumn, with most other flowers gone. The erigeron is then still in full production, covered with three-quarter-inch daisies, silvery rose while opening, clear white when fully expanded. Late-season butterflies, a swarm of blues joined by a red admiral and even a monarch, congregate here on this final patch of sum-mer, in the manner that fish will crowd in lingering pools as their watery world sinks toward oblivion.

These are a weeder's thoughts, mulled as I work alone.

Of any mention of the dozens of additional plants in Mike's floral menagerie, I will spare you the longueur. Except for one more, a malicious beauty, *Agave victoriae-reginae*: a rosette of dark green, white-lined leaves the size and shape of daggers, each tipped with a stabber point. This is a most gardener-unfriendly species. It gets me through my gloves every time I weed around it, the ingrate.

Oh yes, I'm helping out with the weeding, and on the whole enjoying it, or not minding it. At the very beginning of our rock garden-cum-rockery project, in my first talk with Mike about it, I tried to make sure he understood that the garden would need hand-weeding every three months at the least. Mike is more of a landscaper than a maintainer (my predilection, as well, if I could get away with it). He doubted his patience as a weeder even before the weeds appeared, but thought he might have an answer: Marge had the calm nature that would suit her admirably to the task. Marge wasn't around just then to join in the conversation, but I heard from Mike later that her answer had been "Think again."

He and I have been elected the weeders, and have managed to keep up, which in our race with weeds means constantly running behind, then dashing forward. Well, it is only another chore, like shaving. There is always the relaxed option of letting the beard and the weeds grow awhile. They get tougher for being left, but the facial terrain or that of the garden can be restored to neatness on a more ambitious day.

10

A Stroller's Garden

As small as it is, ours is a stroller's, or even a hiker's garden, here on Mount Roskill. Within this three quarters of an acre, I have by now laid out more than a thousand feet of pathway and twelve stepways. That, I suppose with some sadness, is about the limit. But I keep looking for one more place to put another path or set of steps, knowing that the greater the pedestrian experience, the more the sensory and intellectual involvement in the garden: The more one perceives at a slow pace, the richer one's responses are. My pathways and stepways bring the person as close to plants as can be. In some places along the paths you encounter plants that have been encouraged to grow a bit forward, so they can tap a leafy hello on your shoulder or arm. Fragrant plants or plants that are feathery soft are best for such proximity. Any kind of stiff branch that would straight-arm the stroller is to be kept back.

Most of the paths and steps here are green-surfaced rather than mineral. The garden paths closest to the house are ribbons of grass, regularly mowed and edged. But in

main part, the fifth of a mile of pathways are covered pleasantly with carpeting weeds of European origin, which form
a path-long mudguard in wet weather and help keep out
coarse, taller invaders. The carpeters that perform these
wonderful services have come of their own volition and joy,
of course, as weeds will do. But what friends they are in
the circumstances.

When new, the paths were slashes of freshly opened
earth winding the hillsides of the property. Soil, newly cut
and leveled in the making of paths, turns to muck when
walked on in rainy weather. Since I could only cut the soil
after it had begun to soften under autumn rains, the resulting mud was a deep problem. My garden gumboots
would sink in above the ankles. I remember having to lift
one foot out of its seized footwear and, while teetering on
the remaining, booted foot, having to use both hands plus
back power to pull out the mired boot. I spread sawdust
five inches deep on the quagmire. Much of it became
kneaded in when I attempted traverse, but a second application of sawdust to fill in my Sasquatch footprints in the
mud gave a walkable surface at last, or rather a navigable
one, as queasy as a waterbed.

The mud problem cured itself with the drying of the
soil early the next summer, and has never returned with
successive autumns of rain. That first year, with the spreading of the sawdust, we had a good-looking path. The second year we had a path of sawdust disappearing, along its
sunnier stretches, beneath mats of lawn daisies, clover,
speedwell, heal-all, and pennyroyal (old English weeds

with old English titles), with shy, or sly, wisps of a thin-bladed grass coming up between those other mat-forming plants. In its third and fourth years, the path turned completely green, with the grass beginning to overwhelm the other plants. At all stages of greening, the appearance of the path is improved by running a lawn mower over it every month or so.

The alternatives to admitting path weeds to your life are to hoe them or poison them, and then sow in their stead a fine grass lawn on the path or to spread fresh sawdust or some other topping. But I'm enjoying my paths of weeds; they lend the garden a country-lane aspect of dynamic Nature at your very feet, with bees in the weed flowers, and with that weed butterfly, the cabbage white, along with more distinguished lepidoptera in the blue clan, and the many more secretive forms of small life, all busy at once.

Most of the twelve stepways in this steep garden I've carved out of the native earth, using a spade as a shaping tool. Once formed, the steps did not long remain bare earth. The good weeds arrived, here as on the paths, to cover and hold the shaped earth. On the sunnier steps, wild grass predominates, qualifying the structures as turf steps (a known term in gardening). In part shade, others among my weed workers clothe and hold the stepways. One set of steps in full shade is now a moss garden, which began as airborne spores; in the moss carpet grow several species of native ferns, also arrivistes.

Another of the earthen stepways is a garden altogether

planted (a design I'll describe later on). Still others are of stone. And one set is made of railroad ties. The anomaly of this milled material in a garden where all the other stepways are naturalistic may be reasonably justified in that the steps extend from a bridge across the creek, where I've used railroad ties as bridge railings.

Turf steps are evidently an old idea in garden-making, but have never been, as far as I can gather, a commonplace. A fine historical example of turf steps, now nearly 150 years old, is to be seen in the Moffat-Ladd Garden in Portsmouth, New Hampshire. This sesquicentenarian stepway of thick grass lives on — eight broad, even steps, saved by the grass from rain erosion, frost action, and hammering footfalls. Grass is a great preserver of sculpted soil. Even millennia-old Celtic soil terracing in Britain, protected by pasture grass, appears freshy carved, as do centuries-old Maori earthworks, secured by the greensward on Auckland's mounts.

The soil supporting my turf steps is a firm loam, laid down by Nature and anciently cohesive, a help to the grass in retaining the crisp evenness of the steps. At age thirteen, the steps take care of themselves — except for turning shaggy with the full-length growth of the grass during my months of absence. When I'm here, and if I am in one of my determinedly neat modes of gardening, I find time to keep them hand-clipped.

On another garden slope, where the ground was mainly rock rubble, unstable for step-making, I gouged a rough shoot in the hillside, then filled it and formed it into a stairway of rock rubble mixed with clay. I mined the clay in a distant corner of the garden, on this property where a complex soil profile has been exposed by the deep cutting of the creek over a period of thousands of years. After shoveling the clay into a wheelbarrow, I added just enough water with the garden hose to make a stiff potter's clay of it, workable with effort. An investment of several afternoons went into the digging, hauling, kneading, and sculpting (with slapping blows of spade blade and hammering with booted foot) of sufficient clay and rock to form ten two-foot-wide steps on a forty-five-degree hillside.

Having sculpted the steps, I carpeted them, while the clay was still moist, with that infamous lawn weed of Europe, North America, and New Zealand, *Veronica filiformis* (a haze of about a million tiny violet flowers in the grass in springtime); I had gathered the plant from half-shady nooks in the garden, where it grew in pure colonies as much as a yard across. I'm an admirer of this veronica in gardens, have never resented its sharing of ground with lawn grass, and have always encouraged its clothing ability on patches of bare earth or concrete. The threadlike roots of the plant spread shallowly in the soil — more shallowly still, of course, on concrete — allowing the gardener to skin away the foliage mat and root mass with a spade and replant it as a green ruglet.

I draped such ruglets over the steps, pressing the root mass into the moist clay. Completed with this carpeting, the steps were not yet ready for hard use. For weeks I stepped gingerly upon them, until such time as the clay dried and hardened and the carpeting plant took hold firmly. (An even better choice for a carpeter would have been *Laurentia fluviatilis,* hardy nearly to zero, available from nurseries, tougher and more traffic-resistant on steps than the veronica, which I used simply because I had it for free.)

The veronica steps were an experiment that has worked about 85 percent satisfactorily. Twelve years on, time has brought changes to the layout. Benign little weeds of other species have invited themselves, supplanting much of the veronica. Not to worry. The idea was to have protective plants covering the steps, and these interloping weeds have worked just as well, although not perfectly. The steps have bowed a little under the weight of people passing this way in wet weather, when the clay is soft. I could easily enough restore them to ruler-straight lines by adding clay. However, I too am twelve years along, and more apt to let well enough alone.

A more elaborately planted earthen stepway in our garden forms a composition I call Carex Cascade. The main plant here is New Zealand's *Carex albula,* in habit a silvery green clump of sedge, arching downward of foliage. With its silvery plunge of slender-bladed leaves, this plant has always reminded me of the flow of mountain brooks. I've planted it to bear out the suggestion. With willing suspension of disbelief, the hiker negotiates rapids, that is, the clumps of the *Carex* as white water.

On the steps alongside the *Carex* grow hummocks of *Tolmiea menziesii,* better known as the house plant youth-on-age; also a soil-hugging ground cover, the softly green *Isotoma fluviatilis,* aforementioned as being especially resilient under foot pressure. (Division and redivision of one plant purchased at a garden center provided in three years' time all the stock of the plant I could ever use.) I somewhat control the *Isotoma*'s spread on the step treads, which seem to need the visual stabilization of soil in view.

The make-believe cascade actually became one on a certain day, by one of those little miracles that take place in any garden, incidents such as the arrival of a splendid, unexpected butterfly or bird or person, or an exultation of foliages and flowers in a companionship never planned by the gardener. But this miracle came in the form of water.

On a certain day, the Carex Cascade liquefied, almost before my very eyes. The happening took place in the late afternoon, following two days of exceptionally heavy rain. The sun came out, cuing my own emergence from the house. I set out on a trek of the garden paths, eager to join a silvery world of sun reflecting from wet leaves, and also, I must confess, to boggle in boyish awe at the rare ferocity of the usually docile and silent little stream that runs through the bottom of the garden, that day one long tyrannosaurian roar.

Rounding a bend in the path, I came to the base of the *Carex* steps and discovered them to be cascading not only with silvery leaves but with a flow of clear water. From a spring that had never before appeared in my presence, the water ran clean, without eroding a particle of the clayey earth of the steps. The plants guarded the soil. Stigmatically, it seemed, water freshened from a small opening in the ground at the top of the steps, flowed evenly down over them as if they had been designed to receive it, and on down to join the roar below.

The water subsided within hours. The aperture closed, disappeared. I dug into the ground looking for a channel, but found nothing. Nor have I ever again seen that freshet, however heavy the rainfall. No matter. My miniature falls flow quite as satisfactorily in memory as the great cascade in Chatsworth Garden. I think I like mine even better.

11

Pausing to
Look at Leaves

THIS COUNTRY is famous in the world of horticulture rather more for extraordinary foliages than for flowers. In our garden are numbers of New Zealand foliage plants of such comely attractiveness, or of such diabolical beauty, I'm forever pausing along the paths, held for long moments by leaves.

The glistening leaves of *Coprosma repens* catch the eye like a mirror in sunlight; the species is in fact called mirror plant in California, where it is becoming popular in home landscaping. New Zealanders know the shrub by its Maori name, taupata. The natural plant is a rich, polished green. The species is given to freaking into goldish or silvery leaf variegations, preferred by most gardeners.

In the case of lemonwood (*Pittosporum eugenioides*), I pause not only to look but to pick a sprig of the crinkly yellow-green leaves on their branchlet with its black-rose bark. Rolled between the fingers, the leaves give up a lemony aroma so true to the fruit that it puckers the mouth. Nature must have recognized that it had produced masterpieces of perfumery in the citrus scents, lemon and orange, for so many different plants, from trees and shrubs down to perennials, are embued with them. Lemonwood has become one of the better-known New Zealanders in California and the Southwest of the United States. It makes an accommodating screening or hedge plant, with wood fairly easy to cut back, even with hand tools, as I do.

Coprosma virescens, with its tiny leaves on wiry branches, typifies New Zealand's many shrubs of ramifying habit. Pioneer New Zealanders, traveling on foot or horseback, sleeping out, used these springy plants as mattresses. I've tried a lie-back on several of the meshwork species of *Coprosma* and *Muehlenbeckia* growing on coastal slopes, and find them yielding yet resilient. They support your weight with the fine consideration an inner-spring mattress has for the body's bumps and hollows — no jabbing of the carcass.

Hundreds of different plants in New Zealand have evolved into such springy thickets of tiny leaves on intricate, thin stems, but all the rest of the world has very few species of this character. There is a beautiful, even lovable theory explaining why; lovable, I say, in that it is so easily understandable and manifestly true. New Zealand was the land of moas, birds up to eleven feet tall, with vast appetites for leaves. The ramifying habit of vegetation developed as a defense against the moas, the islands' main herbivores, in a natural economy that contained no land mammals at all. Peck away at the wiry stems and tiny leaves as they would, the moas could not crop a decent beakful. The branches would yield when picked; the leaves were too small to grasp, or were located protectively in the shrub's interior. It is easy to conjure up a scenario from prehistory of the gigantic birds being puzzled in their pea brains by the plant, then moving on to crop the vulnerable tussocks instead.

The foliage of the young *Pseudopanax ferox* (lancewood) is my very favorite for the beauty of the devil. The stiff leaves are arranged as narrow, downward-pointing spokes around a slim spear of a trunk. The juvenile foliage, carried until about the plant's twentieth year, suggests a variety of reptiles: The mottled tan of the leaf is that of the skins of certain snakes and turtles; the narrow, snout-tipped leaf is like the head of the cayman; the spiny leaf edges are as the bristling hide of the horned lizard; the leaf midrib, a stripe of muted orange or red, repeats precisely the color and pattern of the garter snake. Usually by the plant's third decade of life the animalistic leaves of lancewood are replaced with broader foliage of more ordinary, foresty appearance. The devil retreats into the seeds of the plant's black berries and awaits rebirth.

For a more sanctioned beauty, there is the subtle coloration of the leaves of *Pseudowintera colorata,* although again, there is in them an ingredient of strangeness, the hallmark of these islands. The *Pseudowintera* is a choice (that is, slow-growing), shapely shrub usually only a few feet high after many years in the garden. It is an evergreen, as is virtually every one among the thousands of native New Zealand plants. The wavy-margined leaves, through their first year, are veined, spotted, and suffused with wine rose, almost masking the pale brown mother color of the foliage. Second- and third-year leaves, carried in the interior of the shrub, are of that pale brown, now with a leaf rim vinous black, the color of a pinot noir grape. The underside of all the leaves, new and old, is a powdery silver-violet.

The intensity of the coloration in the new leaves varies from individual to individual in this species. Plain tan dullards show up in any lot of seedlings. Nursery selection and vegetative propagation will be needed to place this shrub where it belongs horticulturally, as one of the prouder plants in the collector's garden.

However singular each species, New Zealand's cornucopia of foliages blend with startling appropriateness into a grand harmony. The 15 percent of the country's land area still in its natural state remains a symphonic plant composition containing exactly the right selection and number of notes. No gardener could ever improve on natural plant composition as rich as this.

The earlier Britons to come here saw it all very differently. The strangeness of New Zealand's foliages seemed repellent to the settlers in the nineteenth and early twentieth centuries. The bush (the forest, the coastal chaparral) was the enemy, to be felled, slashed, and burned back, and certainly not to be considered a source of candidates for the garden. Britons at heart, even to the third and fourth generations in the antipodes, New Zealanders thought of England as the mother country and a trip to England as "going home." Proper garden plants came from England, or from anywhere but the new land.

Such an attitude of alienation prevailed until a wave of down-home pride arose in the 1970s. New Zealand has lately embarked on an intense search for itself, surely in part out of a sense of having lost its mother, in a severing of ties of trade. The newer New Zealand has shown up in gardens, in a sudden appreciation of native plants by most of the public. In theory at least, the country might easily develop a nationalistic garden, as Japan did centuries ago, utilizing only native plants. Japan worked with a relatively limited botanical repertory; its classical gardens employed only a few score cultivable plants, albeit these were se-lected, during centuries of nursery work, into thousands of leaf, stem, and flower forms. New Zealand has, at the start, thousands of usable native plants at its garden com-mand. These can be composed into landscape adventures like those of no other country.

A few home gardeners here explore such ethnic routes, creating gardens purely of native plants. Their example, however, seems unlikely to be repeated sufficiently ever to prevail as a national style: the garden of New Zealandic leafage. The time for that has passed, with a reductive world's regional garden art blending into a vegetative blancmange rather than confirming itself nation by nation.

For my part, in my appreciation of leaves, I'm a dedi-cated eclectic, a gardener-gatherer of foliages from every-where. In fact, the world geography of the garden, as that of philately, is for me one of its constant features of interest. My recent purchase (out of flower, flower unknown to me), for foliage value alone, of a mound of bold, lined lance-blade leaves named *Echium fastuosum* — in English, the pride of Madeira — brought me once again the voyager's excitement in gardening, dropping anchor at a port of call I've never known before.

12

Mount
Suburbia

MOUNT ROSKILL SUBURB, locus of our garden, extends over hills that were in the nineteenth century a dense subtropical forest of kauri, totara, and other timber trees. Logged off, pastured, the undulant land became a prairie ocean of openness. With the arrival of the suburb, the hills have become waves on which flotillas of cottages bob up and down, few in sight anchored by a garden.

The vision is hypnotic, soporific — and pandemic. Mount Roskill is only one of the ten thousand or so most visually boring, barren suburbs in the world. I have a feeling I must have seen all the other nine thousand nine hundred ninety-nine candidates. I even experience at times an ominous déjà vu of having lived in them all. In fact I have lived and gardened in quite a number.

And I note that the ungardeny barrenness of communities becomes a kind of neighborhood tyranny, self-perpetuating decade after decade. Newcomers look around to see what the neighbors have done (next to nothing) and decide to keep down with the Joneses. The relative affluence of neighborhoods has less to do with richness of land-scaping than neighborhood attitude does. Sometimes whole communities of modest homes join together in a visual agreement to landscape for a better life, that is, a garden life somewhat protected from public view, leafy and shady, sunny just right, and colorful with flowers. Who starts the community on this track? At times, someone brave.

Steve, a gardener I know, decided to enclose his front yard, a grass patch, with handsomely designed cedar pan-eling to make a livable outdoor room for trees, shrubs, pot plants, and children. (The back yard, a downslope, could have been made livable only by decking it over, at pro-hibitive cost.) Neighborhood reaction to his front yard up-graded to garden appeared in notes tacked to the cedar paneling, condemning his audacity in spoiling the unifor-mity of the street full of open front yards. But then, ana-lyzing the benefits, other householders on the street began to screen their front yards, converting them into garden rooms. Now it is quite the thing in the neighborhood.

My own task as a suburban gardener has always been to make the small place commodious and homelike. The making of Home Sweet Home in a small garden depends first of all on screening at least a portion of the property from public view, architecturally or greenly, and then de-signing within it a space for living. The true garden must contain at least one outdoor room private enough for one to shuffle about scandalously, perhaps to lounge, still a sleep-sodden thing, in one's nightclothes on a fine morning, and while there to say hello to a sufficient number of resident plant friends.

In suburban Auckland I have, besides plants, other, even steadier friends in Nature: a collection of volcanic hills — mounts, as they are called here — a mile or more separate from each other, unique to this city. My home suburb on Mount Roskill joins other suburbs, which cover the flanks of other mounts. At the beginning of European immigration, there were more than forty volcanoes in the Auckland area. Now there are fewer than twenty. Some have been nearly erased in the quarrying of their stone. Others are fairly pristine conical shapes a few hundred feet high. The mounts are geologically new, a mere few thousand years old. Yet the lava of the slopes has broken down into a rich red-brown soil. In past centuries, local Maori tribes set up villages on the mounts, having found the volcanic slopes excellent for growing sweet potatoes and advantageous in combating murderous invaders. Then, early in the European era, the mounts were sown to pasture, and now on their upper slopes blackpoll cattle pull at the grass, as oblivious as gardeners pulling weeds.

The city's now-quiet little Vesuviuses arise as grassy redoubts above surrounding, besieging cottages. The land on top and on upper slopes is reserved for public use, with access roads spiraling the volcanic cones. Joggers, bicyclists, and hikers get a good workout here. The upthrust land is beneficial also just for the viewing. These conical hills must rank among the most affecting sculpture of any in the midst or the province of the world's cities. They are as oddly, provocatively present as the great sand cone in the garden of Kyoto's Silver Pavilion. They offer the spirit a redemptive lift remindful of those heavenly antennas the Watts Towers, in suburban Los Angeles. In mass and shape, Auckland's volcanoes approximate the Great Pyramids (now beset by the sprawl of Cairo), and they further resemble those manmade mounts in being vaults of time, manifest thousands of years that help quieten any nagging sense that tempus fugit.

Cottager that I am, located on a lower, populous slope of Mount Roskill, I have two quick escapes from suburbia open to me. Say that I am fed up with gardening at the moment — I might take a hike to Mount Roskill's summit, a not-too-difficult grade, and only a mile distant. Or say that I am intrigued with the garden just now, but not with gardening. In this instance I will make my most frequent escape, simply by strolling in the garden with a Zen-like concentration on its minutiae — a leaf, a bud, a bloom, a pleasant insect — a serene ceremonial that takes me out of the human community, effectively evaporating its very existence for the interval.

Gardeners are shrewd and lucky and blessed — conditions that follow in a line — in having made for themselves another inhabitable world close to home. Those homeowners who have not made garden worlds for themselves are forced to spend a great deal more of their soul-saving time away from home. There is a perceptible rule governing suburban leisure time: the less garden, the more need to get in the car and go.

Each weekend this dictate leads to a mass migration from Mount Roskill. The place becomes so deserted on a balmy summer Sunday, the only life being the music of cicadas cued by the warmth of the sun, a day-long trill of toy whistles punctuated by castanet *click-clicks*, incessant yet soothing — so lonely, except to a gardener relishing solitude — that lately I have been approached by a neighborhood cat desperate for companionship. It comes from . . . nowhere, from what weekend-abandoned property I don't know. The creature approaches at a passionate trot, mewing a *pobrecito mio* plaint. A stroke of my hand along the dark gray back turns mewing to purring. Quite a handsome animal, this, of a short-haired breed I have heard called British Blue. Responding to my gaze, the cat looks up, eyes pale agate in the sun, dreamily distant. Sometimes my Sunday friend will then lie down in the sun's warmth, near me while I work, or sit on haunches, staring fixedly at my planting of *Nepeta* 'Six Hills Giant'.

This *Nepeta,* with its tallish stems of smoky gray-violet summer flowers and cat-entrancing aroma, is one of the several forms of catnip. The British Blue (and other neighborhood cats, who skulk here at night) would certainly mawl and chew and barrel-roll upon the plant until it was in bits if I didn't provide protection. To keep the beasts at bay, I back the *Nepeta* with taller perennials and plant in front of it perennials that are somewhat shorter (*Carex,* lady's mantle, chamomile, and others). The planting in front is short enough not to obscure the *Nepeta*'s flowers and tall enough to deter the connoisseurs. Cats, as you've probably observed, are trail animals who prefer clear, safe pathways and passages and avoid rough, possibly entangling vegetation, except in the transport of pouncing on animal prey.

Ensconced on a path of mown grass that outlines the bed where the *Nepeta* grows, the gray cat will sit for some minutes, staring at the plant with the coolness of any feline regarding an idling fish in the water, waiting for an unwise move. I trust in my surrounding planting to discourage the catnip from venturing forward into the reach of the cat and the cat from braving the bulwark of vegetation. It works. The peace of the garden prevails.

13

Coming Home

HOME IS WHERE the garden grows. Onward now to four more gardens that I visit on my yearly rounds, each a place of unique horticultural and human friendships, as of course any garden develops into being.

Elva's garden is a balance of foliages and flowers that we set up in containers each spring on a terrace just outside the paraplegic ward at Lion's Gate Hospital in North Vancouver, where Elva is a patient. This yearly garden is the brainchild of Candida, a friend of Elva's and mine. We began in the spring of 1984, on a bleakly empty concrete terrace defined by a four-foot concrete wall. Neither Elva nor any of the other residents in the ward ever took the air or received visitors on this grim gray plateau. Instead, they remained indoors, confining themselves to the ward's corridor. Now, with the garden in place, often as many as five and occasionally as many as ten residents at once, along with family members and friends, congregate on the terrace in nice weather.

Candida broached this garden on the terrace in the

same manner I began my garden within the walls of Manila, that is, without asking anybody but with the sense that a garden should be here, where there was only blankness. Once it was in place, the hospital's authorities saw the harmlessness and healthfulness in the project and welcomed it. Candida and I give the congregation of viewers all the plant variety, in amounts scaled down to fit the confines of the terrace, of a fully furnished home garden growing in the open ground. We place tubbed conifers in a line to form background greenery; pots of annual and perennial flowers; tea roses chosen for scent, and rose of Sharon in several colors; ferns and *Nandina* nestled in the shade of the wall; sweet peas and edible peas, sown to climb simple frames of string and lumber nailed to planters; and, among a few other vegetables, differing in variety from year to year, tomatoes recurrently.

The tomato plant not only pays off in edibility, it performs as the greatest of season markers while we wait. The gravidity of the plant, a process of stately slow measure, etches the days of summer on our senses better than any other edible or flower on the terrace: We are here, gardeners and garden watchers, part of summer's festival once again. We also become the tomato plant's expectant uncles and aunties in our observance of little star-eye flowers of soft yellow, which transmute to hard green marbles, then patiently expand to a white-green planetary fullness; and at last the reddening comes, when it will come. To gain the full performance, I must carefully choose the earliest varieties — "55 days," "62 days" — for in the predominantly cool, untomatoey summer of the Pacific Northwest, the actual time of ripening fruit seldom comes before about 120 days, no matter what the promise on the label.

The terrace's wall top is the garden's prime platform for viewing, for which I always pot up, in our best-looking ceramic, a few uncommon plants of striking form or color, such as *Ephedra, Equisetum,* and the oxblood red grass, *Imperata cylindrica* 'Rubra'. These plants provide drama and elegance, and attract the most curiosity of any of the garden's displays, a collective "Hmmm" from our audience.

Our audience, I say, considering that we have in this garden a theater in the round. Any gardening activity — potting, grooming, rearranging of containers — will bring a circle or semicircle of onlookers, intent and silent, in wheelchairs drawn closely about. I recognize their sense of participation, for I myself am an avid watcher of gardeners at work on TV gardening shows.

One other person figures in the algebra of Elva's garden: her husband, Bob. Theirs, by the way, is a story of monogamy for the book of records. Childhood neighbors in the 1920s, they have been sweethearts since grade school days, and neither ever dated anybody else. Bob, a retired railroad engineer (thirty-eight years at the throttle of a transcontinental locomotive), visits Elva at Lion's Gate from 10:30 to 1:30 and again from 4:00 until 8:00 every day of the year, and he waters the garden just as unfailingly during the days of summer.

Lately Bob has protected the garden from squirrels. These were always animals in the middle distance on the hospital grounds until recently, when several people among the garden's regulars began placing peanuts and other seeds on the terrace floor to coax the squirrels up close. They quickly responded, and then went on the dole as a way of life, mooching about just outside the terrace, waiting for largess. On dull, chill days, with the garden empty of people and provender, the squirrels grew frustrated and riotous. They took to attacking the pot plants, scratching up the soil in a search for food (perhaps a peanut they'd stashed), and kicking any new plants completely out of their pots. Bob's remedy: mothballs placed on the surface of the soil — three, for example, to an eighteen-inch, bowl-shaped pot of petunias. Mothballs have totally turned away the bushy-tailed little beggars. The method is evidently time-honored hereabout, a means Bob learned from local gardeners who have been using it at least since the 1920s to keep squirrels away from vegetables growing in open ground. But it is the brightest of news to me, a garden saver this summer.

Come autumn, Bob the Handy can be counted on to help put the garden to bed. Lion's Gate has allocated to us an obscure patch of soil in its landscaped grounds, into which we heel all the garden's hardy plants for the winter. Before planting, we root-prune (we, or Bob and Candida alone, if I'm not in town), cutting back roots by about one third so that each specimen will fit into the same container next summer, with room to spare for an addition of fresh soil. Pruning shears are the requisite tool, except in the case of the garden's conifers, *Thuja occidentalis* 'Fastigiata'.

To the roots of these trees — they are actually more green columns, living modules of architecture — we apply a stoutly bladed butcher knife, a kitchen machete, slicing away about three inches from the sides and the bottom of the root mass. These supremely tough and hardy tree columns never feel distressed, or if they do, never show it. They will return reliably in new leaf next year, they and the garden's other heeled-in plants.

While I follow the sun southward — I trust this is not hateful news to my possibly chilblained reader — I entertain northerly thoughts of all these plants wintering, slumberously nurturing new roots, like a bear with newborn cubs, deep in a den for the winter.

My mental pictures of plants I've placed in gardens around the world form quite a stack of snapshots, which I go through for comfort and a sense of riches, as a boy will leaf through his pile of baseball cards, or, I suppose, as a poxy old pervert will pore over his collection of pornographic snapshots (in writing of plants and gardens, a dash of vinegar helps cut the sweetness inherent in the subject matter). A favorite plant portrait I carry is of *Miscanthus sinensis* 'Silver Feather' growing in Nancy's garden. Nancy, an editor by profession, is one of my original garden hosts. Since the early 1960s, I've shared with my friend divisions and rootings of plants I've grown, and have found compatible places for them in her garden on the shore of Lake Washington in the Puget Sound country.

Miscanthus sinensis, the parental species that gave rise to
the garden seedling 'Silver Feather', is surely one of the
world's great image plants, none other than that tall, reedy
grass portrayed in Japanese scrolls, with its gray seed
plumes of gracefully arching habit. There in the plant's
homeland, people travel to the countryside expressly to see
this grass in autumn plume. It is one of Japan's anciently
admired "viewing plants," with which people of classical
taste mark the season on the calendar of the senses (just as
we of Elva's garden employ the tomatoes of summer).

The seedling selection 'Silver Feather' (the name is a
translation of 'Silber Feder', given by the originating nursery, in the Netherlands, as I recall) offers the garden advan-
tage of surely flowering in Europe and North America,
where the parent plant usually lacks the verve for full flowering because of summers less balmy than those of its native Asia. 'Silver Feather' became available in the 1970s
and, as will happen in these years of swift worldwide dis-
tribution of exciting new plants, earned immediate fame.
Graham Stuart Thomas, in his masterful book *Perennial
Garden Plants,* published in 1976, calls 'Silver Feather'
"one of the greatest delights of the September garden.
Beautiful with late monkshood."

In Nancy's garden, this clump-forming grass stands
alone, seven feet tall in gray granitic sand, its plumy seeds
atop their straight, firm stems repeating the mineral color
but also catching the light of autumn sun and giving back
a silky sheen. 'Silver Feather' grows vigorously, hydroponi-
cally, in sand at the lakeshore, plunging roots down below

the water table and availing itself of a constant supply of nutritious lakewater. The lake, nearly still on calm days, nibbles at the sand with minnow lips of water close by the plant's base. No other vegetation stands near. The great grass clump, the sand, and the water are the total scene.

That's but a momentary truth. If I stand there viewing the plumy grass more than two minutes, the lake's Canada geese, malingerers diverted from their southward migration by easy pickings, will sail into shore, waddle up to me, and grab at my pants leg with their clapshoe bills, thuggishly demanding a handout.

Invasive animals seem to be moving in from all sides in this writing, as startling as a manifestation of aphids on a stem. I hadn't planned the intrusions; they're just happening. You will remember the cat and the catnip in the garden at Mount Roskill. Encore the whole business, now relocated seven thousand miles north.

While still in New Zealand, I ordered a parcel of perennials, including that same cat madness, *Nepeta* 'Six Hills Giant', from a mail-order nursery in the United States, and had the order sent to my mother and stepfather, who live near Seattle. I'm always sending or taking them plants. My folks, both of whom were born in June 1902, remain active gardeners. While he has always been a planter and a propagator, my mother's contribution has never included these engendering aspects of gardening. Instead, she is a weeder, actually for enjoyment ("That's when I get some of my best thinking done"), a keen harvester of flowers for the house, and a merciless deadheader of perennials in the autumn. My mother is part French, and I suspect her of being a sympathetic descendant of some guillotine hobby-ist of the Madame Defarge type. In vain I beg that the attractive brown seed heads of *Astilbe, Carex, Tovara,* and *Centaurea* be allowed their rightful afterlife.

That issue comes up yearly in the autumn. The busi-ness this spring was the box of mail-order plants. They came bare-rooted and arrived in fine condition. They might have been planted directly in the garden, with care-ful watering afterward to prevent any flagging until they could send new roots well down. However, my stepfather, Holly, potted them up using a wholesome packaged mix and kept them in his greenhouse for a month, awaiting my return to North America. He preferred for me to do the planting, since he was unfamiliar with these gift plants.

In planting the *Nepeta* 'Six Hills Giant' — and even in ordering it — something important totally slipped my mind: the fact that my parents had lately taken in two young cats, apparent siblings, which had shown up at the door and successfully performed a homeless hardship rou-tine. Now I was to be reminded. Seconds after I planted the *Nepeta* (in a bare patch of ground, with no protective vegetation about — the only place available), one of the cats strode up to it and began harassing it with facial rubs, nosings, and nibblings.

We watched this performance for a moment, Holly, his son Ken, and I, and then got a hammer and some stakes, not to pillory the irksome creature but to pound protective pickets into the ground all around the *Nepeta*. Now the cat commenced rubbing the stakes with its facial scent glands, territorially marking the wood as well as the plant. Ken, a doctor of medicine, remarked solemnly that he had read in some journal that the reaction of cats to catnip is analogous to that of oldtime hippies to marijuana: users, two- or four-legged, soar away into reverie and ecstasy. I'm sure we all reflected awhile on this, Holly, his son, and I; especially Holly.

The next day I stopped by to do some more gardening and found that Holly had wrapped light nylon netting — the kind used as pea vine support — all around the *Nepeta*'s stakes, completely caging the plant in and the cats out. His brow corrugated with concern, he said he didn't know if this plant was going to be such a good idea. Before he had added the netting, Cat 1 had been joined by Cat 2, its shy sibling. Both had been reaching between the stakes to cuff at the plant and tease branches outward for closer nosing and nibbling. Holly said he supposed that if the drugging action of the *Nepeta* was like that of marijuana, it would surely stimulate the libidinous instincts of the cats, a male and a female. He would rather not invite anything of that nature.

I replied, with calm authority, that the marijuana-*Nepeta* analogy was only a writer's colorful invention. The action of catnip on cats was nothing cannabis-like, I assured him. Holly's face smoothed out. What I didn't say was, who knows? *I* certainly didn't. Even as I spoke, I was listening to my conscience: "You haven't the faintest idea what you're talking about."

Bothered, I went to a library as soon as I could and delved into *The Book of the Cat*. I read that the ingestion of catnip evokes in cats physical responses that are "probably unrelated to sexual behavior." The evidence given is that cats of *both* sexes, and either neutered or intact, will roll about on *Nepeta* plants in postures well known to be part of cat coquetry, but no cats have been observed actually coupling while under the influence of the plant. (So there are Masters and Johnsons of catkind, too, clinically spying, scribbling notes. But of course there are, as I surmise from my career of TV watching. I've always been keen on wild-life documentaries, and have paid for it in being an unwitting voyeur of everything in the world, from fruit bats to crabs to kangaroos, in flagrante delicto. These images can never be erased from the mind.) *The Book of the Cat* goes on to say, "It seems that a true psychedelic state is induced by nepetalactone [the active chemical in catnip] reaching the brain. Cats have been observed sitting and staring at infinity, or seen chasing phantom mice. The same bio-chemical pathways are affected by the smell of catnip as by marijuana or LSD, though fortunately the effect is short-lived, non-addictive, and quite harmless." Sounds good. I'll take it all on as much faith as good old Holly accorded my pronouncement on the subject. But really, who knows what secrets dance behind the millefiori irises of a cat's gaze?

About twelve weeks have passed since we planted, palisaded, and netted the *Nepeta* 'Six Hills Giant'. It is now mid-August, the dozy days of summer. The plant seems to have reached full growth, out through and up above the protective covering, almost totally concealing it with billowy gray-greenery and gray-violet. The cats still visit the plant, but now only momentarily each morning. Just a deep sniff does for them these days, and then they go on their way. As I do.

✿

"Muriel, my old friend!"

"George, you've come home!"

My perennial garden friend Muriel and I always greet each other with some such grand hello, accompanied by an ursine hug. Muriel is Muriel Fisher of Auckland, doyenne of New Zealand gardeners, this country's Gertrude Jekyll. Not that Miss J was much for mountain trails, or Mrs. F ever a professional designer of gardens. But the self-same spirit — an understanding of the living plant burning green (*vide* Blake's tiger burning bright) and an ability to convey to people the ardor of that green energy — is surely deep-welled in both women.

I've never added any plant of my own to Muriel's garden, an act that would be a carrying of horticultural coals to Newcastle. However, over the years I have pruned trees and shrubs for my friend, laid out a rock garden, and planted shrubbery and perennials that Muriel has propagated or brought home. This effort (along with sessions of weeding by Mo and other friends of Muriel's) goes toward

the shaping up of her property in preparation for its trans-
fer to the city. The council of Auckland's Birkenhead district, location of her home and garden, has for years been
negotiating with Muriel. The city wants to reserve the
Fisher family acreage, most of which, from the time the
first Fisher arrived at the site in the 1890s, has been kept
as a wilderness of wooded ravine and clear-water creek.
Auckland wants to keep it that way and maintain its trails
as nature walks.

Muriel's property is now pressed on several sides by the
locustlike advance of suburbia. Yet of all major cities in the
world, Auckland is perhaps the most considerate in its outward march over the land. It has secured as public parks —
I don't know how many, no doubt well over a hundred —
beaches, fields, woods, and mounts. Will all these remain
safe in the century to come? My friend Bruce and I were
mulling over this question while hiking in the Fisher
woods. As I recall, we reached dour agreement that the
continuing preservation of the city's public lands, sure to
be subject to increasingly seductive offers by developers in
the twenty-first century, will bring about taut tests of civic
conscience and public alertness. Which is probably as self-
evident as saying that the keepers of a henhouse must
guard against weasels.

But the matter went out of focus and vanished into the
distance in a perfect woodland moment, when we stopped
along the trail to examine a crumbling fragment of log
commandeered as a grandstand by a crowd of little orange-
peel–colored mushrooms. Were they, or we, the circus?

214

Recently, over a period of several days, the city sent a crew of convicts, lightly guarded, out to Muriel's property to clear scrub growth from a stretch of hillside between the garden and the woods. Muriel directed the cleanup and got on pretty well with the motley, grizzling crew. But then, Muriel could tame rhinos and wolverines to a reasonable civility, using twenty-five words or less of cajolery.

The convicts cleared an expanse of soil, richly black and inspiring. Muriel went right out to a nursery specializing in native plants and came back with a few shrubs and about sixty gallon-sized specimens of native ornamental grasses and grasslike plants in shades of copper and silver as well as forest green. Then she gave me a call. Would I plant the collection? Answer: You bet.

It was an easy job of design. Grassy plants work readily with shrubbery of almost any kind, as long as the woody plants are enough taller not to be hidden by the tussocks. While I planted, I lamented the absence of an old leafy friend that had always lived where I was working. I supposed that the press-gang landscape crew had rooted it out. The plant was the perennial *Alocasia odora,* a tall taro relative, a six- or seven-footer with leaves big enough to use as an umbrella if a person was caught in a downpour, and the hooded candle flowers of the arum clan, greeny yellow, sweet with a scent that carries on a breeze. *Alocasia odora* was a favorite of nineteenth-century New Zealand gardeners. Imported plants were all they ever wanted in their gardens, and this bold import from continental Asia showed up well in the roughest of stumpy garden spaces hewn out of the woodland. Nowadays the plant is way out of fashion, rare, never offered by nurseries. In fact, the clump in the Fisher garden was the only one I'd ever seen.

For as long as anybody could remember — and longer, supposedly for a hundred years — the leafy giant had stood there in its station at trailside in black, marshy soil. Every springtime when I visited the garden, I would pause admiringly (and covetously) beside it. Time and again I almost asked for a bit of root. Muriel is a gardener constantly in the giving vein, and very quickly would have given that bit and more. But I always stopped myself. The *Alocasia* was the perfect giant for the place. Disturbing it would have been disgraceful: a lessening of perfection, a battering of the foliage, a mud crater left behind, and myself turned halfway into a New Guinea mud man.

While sadly reviewing my acquaintance with the missing *Alocasia,* I carried on planting the grassy plants. With my spade I pierced the soil just where the giant had stood. The blade of the tool sliced through a tuber very like the largest taro you see in the market. Hello, hello? The *Alocasia* was all there, present in many tubers, subterraneously asleep during summer drought, a season when the springtime muck I had always remembered dries in this spot to an easy loam.

But with the coming of autumn and winter rains and the rise of that vast leafage, the plant in its foreground position would be completely wrong for the new garden. I asked Muriel if she would like to have the tubers transplanted. "Oh yes, the *Alocasia,*" she replied. "I knew that

216

you were an admirer. I had the boys leave it for you. Would you like to take it home?"

The plantsman's heart leaped up. In further chat, I learned that Muriel had always detested the *Alocasia* — never her plant, a relic of some ancestral Fisher, yet undeserving of sentiment. She objected to it as an interloper in her garden, and also in the leafy community of New Zealand. Only those plants native to these islands are loved or even accepted by my friend. Whereas Muriel is a bemused liberal in other directions, cheerfully interested in all the races of humankind settled in this country before and after the arrival from Britain of her own Victorian-era ancestors, her attitude toward plants is that of the fiercest of exclusionists — or make that the purest of New Zealand gardeners.

I took home three big bags, each half filled with the hefty tubers. With my spade I wedged openings for them in the muddy banks of the creek at the bottom of the garden, and pressed the tubers into place.

In writing this, I'm sure I feel something of the dirty glee of a bullion burier who pens a message that will, years hence, lead someone clever to hidden ingots, for the *Alocasia* is booty of a floral kind, brought to these islands on a tall ship, planted in a pioneer garden. And I have come by jet a century later to loot it away and secret it in V's within a V of New Zealand (mark those cryptic clues). I will keep and rejoice over my treasure for a time. And then? The admirable thing about such hearties of the plant kingdom as the *Alocasia* is that given the least chance, they will outlive gardens and gardeners. To whoever may inherit this *Alocasia* of my keeping: Give it a luscious moist spot in part shade and the respect owed to a splendid survivor.

Now that the matter comes to mind, I myself may be about due for at least honorable mention as a garden relic, a desiccated rhizome of some sort, nevertheless with a burning, scheming spark of life safe within. My long, eventful horticultural journey happily continues, for a garden is never finished if the gardener takes care to see that it is not. Who would ever want to have nothing more to do in the garden, no new plants to install and study, no experimental compositions to make? The gardener gardens on, with a curiosity as compelling as that of a robin scratching at the earth.